Liza Carbe and Jean-Pierre Durand bring together more than 30 years of hands-on touring, composition, and production know-how into their new program,

THRIVE AND SURVIVE IN THE MUSIC BUSINESS

The co-founders of the "world guitar" group Incendio show you how to self-book your act, how to attend booking conferences, how to set up your promo materials, how to start recording yourself, how to understand your royalties, and more. The duo have had their compositions placed in hundreds of TV shows and films, and with Incendio they have hit the Billboard charts and achieved over 100 million streaming plays.

Learn how to take control of your career from pros who live it every day!

"The music business is more complicated than ever. Artists have to learn so many aspects that the record companies used to talke care of. It's a completely different world. Liza and JP have made that transition, by learning so many facets of the biz in real time. If you've got your music together and want to bring it to the world, they can help you recognize the pitfalls and the genuine opportunities. They are the real deal."
- Barry Squire: Music Talent Scout, Musicians Institute Staff

THRIVE AND SURVIVE IN THE MUSIC BUSINESS

by

Liza Carbé

and

Jean Pierre Durand

Strange Tree Productions
2020

Table of Contents

This book is dedicated to our partner in Incendio, Jim Stubblefield, as well as Tim Curle and all our former bandmates, and all of the wonderfully talented folks who have become our friends on the road and have lived these pages with us.

Thanks to Mark Barnwell for all his technical skill with our websites, EPK, and general good humor. Thanks to Brittany Frompovich for her editing and clarity, Jenn Cary, Tommy Morgan Jr., Leah Finkelstein, Danna Aliano, Elisabeth Oei, Lindsay Tomasic, Wendie Colter, Lynn Cooper, Bob Stane, Joe Carbe, and the late great Richard Ruse. Thanks to Rocio Durand for her patience and great meals!

Also a thank you to our endorsees who have been so helpful through the years:
MTD Basses
Audio Technica
Savarez Strings
Ampeg
Kenny Hill Guitars
Mackie
EAW

Some websites to check out:
thriveandsurviveinmusic.com
carbeanddurand.com
incendioband.com
jimstubblefield.com
markbarnwell.co.uk
ladybassmusic.net (Brittany Frompovich)
gridd.com (Joe Carbe)

INTRODUCTION – WHY DID WE WRITE THIS?

There are so many books available on the business of music, music production, and social media promotion. All of these are very important in their specialized fields. If you are a musician that just wants to get out there and play, and you don't want to wait around to find the right agent to book you, then you need to understand how to book yourself and where to find the necessary resources. What we have seen repeatedly in our work mentoring and teaching other musicians about booking, touring and royalties is lack of understanding on each of these topics.

We are unique in that we are both touring artists, AND we write music for music libraries, TV, and film, as well as produce other artists.

After 25 years of producing music and 20 years of booking our original bands around the world, we have an informed and realistic understanding of what it takes. None of us learned these skills in college. You may get some of them in school now, but it's all theoretical until you start doing it for real. This book is not designed to be comprehensive – it's more about how we have done business and what we feel may work best.

I have my degree in music from CSUN with emphasis on classical guitar, and JP has his degree in Economics from UC Berkeley. We did learn some invaluable skills in college, which have served us well. However, the techniques we have learned about booking our band and understanding royalty streams, we had to learn on our own. The self-education is constant, as new media always rewrites the rules every few years. We learned techniques by jumping in and asking questions and making mistakes along the way. If we had both known then what we know now, perhaps our career and knowledge base would have been acquired in a less bumpy way! We also could have taken more advantage of the opportunities that we had. But we have no regrets. It's the process of falling down and picking yourself up again that really drives a point home. We have spent quite a bit of time mentoring artists over the years on all these different aspects of the music business. Sometimes people would ask us for help on booking their group, others wanted to understand how royalties worked, and some wanted to know how to promote the album that they just finished recording with us or someone else. All of the issues we will discuss are important to take time to learn and practice to understand and implement.

Besides touring, performing, producing, and writing for our group Incendio, both JP and I also write production music as well as produce other artists. Our path to mentoring other artists started after we would finish producing someone's album and they would ask us, "what do I do now?"
It can be a paralyzing question and has been to a few friends and clients. We would often sit down with them and coach them on the next step. Most often, they would do none of what we told them, so their wonderful music would go unheard except for a few family members, friends, and limited fans. It was sad,

and I think they were inclined to do the work, but we think the task ultimately seemed too daunting.

Other times, a friend or client would tell us about a song they had placed in a movie or show (or with another artist) and had no idea how they were going to collect royalties. Many were seasoned music veterans but knew nothing about any part of the music business that didn't have to do with performance or whatever area in which they worked. Although we were concerned about them, we weren't surprised. We had both been there! The difference was that we had both taken the time to educate ourselves. We had done the work needed to understand as many aspects of the music business as we could.

Over the years of touring with Incendio, we started meeting a few artists that were touring and promoting themselves in the same way we were. We started helping each other; we'd share contacts with them and promote the other band to venues that we are booking for ourselves. With some artists, we have weekly strategy sessions and encourage one another. The process often inspires new ideas and, at the very least, keeps everyone on track and encouraged. There is always a small group of musicians that are self-motivated and willing to do the work. So you should understand right away that there is lots of work involved in booking and managing your own group, but the rewards are many.

It is mandatory to understand your royalties if you are writing music that you want to place in media or with other artists. If you are on Spotify, Pandora, or any other streaming platforms, you also need to understand who pays you and for what you are being paid. Are they paying you as a writer, publisher, owner of the master, or for being the featured artist? So there is this small group of musicians that understands how this all works and a large group that doesn't. Yikes -not good.

Now, many of the musicians that struggle on the business side are excellent at their music craft. They are good songwriters, great performers; they play well and have beautiful voices. The bottom line is that the world would be a better place with those artists' work circling around the globe. But . . . it isn't circling! We saw a need for education and breaking things down so that musicians could be more empowered to be successful at their craft.

Finally, we decided to formalize all this coaching we were doing and write it down in a book. We continue to coach one on one or in groups but thought that having a book to reference all the material along with our podcasts might garner a higher artist success rate. Whether you are an independent musician or you are on a label and have the benefit of team support, you should understand all aspects of the business.

All musicians should understand the different types of royalties and how they are getting paid. There are legions of musicians that have gotten screwed because they didn't understand anything about the business of royalties. These are musicians that are signed to a label, and to the average person looking in on them, that musician is successful. However, if someone else is taking care of all aspects of an artist's business and that person is dishonest, you, the artist, is in a compromised position.

On the other hand, some believe that they should be making more than they are earning, and accuse others of ripping them off when in reality they don't understand anything about royalties and how they work. It's challenging and complicated, but it's the business that you chose, so you need to educate yourself about the business you are in. If you choose to remain ignorant, then you are setting yourself up to be taken advantage of. There's a long sad history of musicians and artists getting screwed, but there have always been those few that choose to prevent disaster by educating themselves.

Remember that just because you may be working with a label or a company that is taking care of everything now, it DOESN'T mean that it is going to be forever. If you are that small percent that has a career that never wanes and you always have a team that you trust and can rely on, well, celebrate you! You can hire us to play at some of your parties! But if you are not in that one percent, then knowing how all aspects of the business work will help you to regroup and continue working when that one gig ends.

We meet musicians all the time that can't see past the old paradigm. The idea of booking him or herself or learning how to produce their own music doesn't even register. If they don't have a record deal and an agent, they don't work. That is sad and not necessary! Too many musicians have had their dreams broken into pieces. Most of these artists were and are incredible performers and writers. Their music deserves to be heard. Even with all the tools that are now available to musicians to take control of their destiny, people still get buried by their own willful ignorance or fear. But you can learn! You WILL make mistakes. You will occasionally get screwed. But you can and will right the ship and chart your individual course.

So here it is. We are going to spell it out for you and give you the tools that you need and the strategies that we use. The rest is up to you.

THE MINDSET BEHIND THIS BOOK

Let's start by saying we don't have all the answers but are familiar with the initial questions!! If you are reading this book or utilizing the website, the chances are that you, like us, either want to avoid the standard manager/agent paradigm OR you have already been down that road, OR no one is thus far interested in doing all this work for you.

We, as Incendio, have worked for 20 years under the ethos "make the market." Find out where your music fits, and smack it like a railroad spike! The major labels didn't know how to market us – we were and still are the classic "tweener," between world music and jazz, between Latin music and middle eastern, not easily fit into any one category. That used to be a death knell for sales, but we kept at it, through a few different indie labels, to owning almost all our masters and learning how to navigate the world of streaming.

We started in 2000 during the death of the old record label paradigm – record stores were disappearing, Borders Books (long a great bookstore like Barnes and Noble, but one that also featured live bands) which once carried our CD's in their listening stations, was struggling. Also, all the classic CD distribution places that also distributed Incendio's CD's were going out of business. We survived that music business collapse, and were in the weeds, building our brand throughout the years, even through the 2008 recession.

It has been a slow and steady climb to where we are now, having charted in Billboard, having over 101 million spins on Pandora and climbing. But it is a struggle, no doubt. The major labels have taken the reins at streaming services, and it's harder now to yell above the din to get heard. Also, longtime shows like "America's Got Talent" have romanticized and storyboarded the ascent of the singer. But across America, artists who want to get heard and don't fit the paradigm of those outlets, bands who have worked hard to forge their own destinies – folks like Joe Craven, Dirty Revival, Lisa Lynne, Larkin Poe, Eliza Gilkyson, David Jacobs-Strain, Joe Bonamassa, Samantha Fish - an endless list of folks who believe so much in the music that they work a bit "outside" the usual industry paradigm and inspire other like-minded folks who are in the "tribe" of music to follow their hearts. If you're reading this and during that last sentence, you said "that's me!", then you're going to find parts of this book VERY resonant and refreshing.

You will need to get organized. You will learn to roll over mistakes, failures, and rejection, and in the process, your music will become more developed and focused. This is not a road or a business for the weak-hearted. You have to be willing to work exceptionally hard, and possibly put as much work into the business side as you do your own music, but ALWAYS keep a space in your heart for collaboration, for constructive criticism, and for the community of your peers to give support and receive it. We have been "coaching" these attributes for over 20 years, but we didn't know it was "coaching." We thought it was just helping. Now we want to help you, and if you feel you want more support, visit thriveandsurviveinmusic.com to look at a personal coaching program that can help you with EVERYTHING you are about to read.

Chapter 1
The Tools You Need

- Current live videos to show promoters
- Pictures of the group
- Stage Plot
- Bio, both band and individual
- Website with info about the group & social media
- Press, write-ups
- Good recording of your music
- EPK

The first thing you need to do before starting to book yourself or your group is to have something for promoters to hear and see. When you get someone interested in your group, you want to have everything ready. You need recordings of your music, a video, a website that has info about the band, a bio, pictures, and your social media pages.

VIDEOS

You NEED a recording of your music for the promoters to hear, preferably a professional recording. Sometimes that's a studio recording – sometimes it's a live recording. Most promoters want to see some sort of video so they can hear what you sound like live and review your look. Having a concept video for your fans is great, but for booking, you need to have something that shows a live performance. Promoters don't want to be surprised. They need to know that you have played live and know how to put on a good show. Having a good sounding album or song doesn't necessarily translate to a strong live performance.

If you are just starting out, try to record some good live footage on a video camera or iPhone. You can get someone to shoot it for you or get a stand and set it up where it will capture a decent single-camera performance of the group. You also need to consider the sound as well as the video when deciding where to place the camera. If you look great, but the sound quality is bad, the video is not going to help you. If you don't have anyone that can help you shoot a video, then you are going to have to take the time to find the best place to put the camera. This might mean going to a performance at the venue where you are going to be and filming another act. That way, you can shoot in several locations, which will help you find the sweet spot for audio and video. Getting a friend or someone that can help you with this is, of course, a better scenario, but sometimes you just have to improvise. Be aware: finding the sweet spot for the other band doesn't mean that's the best placement for the camera for YOUR group, but it gives you a place from which to start. Having an excellent live video is one of your best tools for getting booked!

Don't assume that the promoter will understand that the PA was subpar, or the iPhone wasn't in an optimal place. They won't! You need to make a great first impression. So practice. Shoot the group practicing. Make sure you have good lighting. Make sure that wherever you place the iPhone or video camera, it's getting good sound.

Doing a multi-camera shoot that you can edit in Final Cut Pro X, Adobe Premiere or iMovie (or any of several other video editing software options) is the next step. You can create movement and make a much more dynamic video with several cameras and editing software.

Whether we are flying or driving, when we tour with Incendio, we pack two cameras (old trusty Canon Vixias, shooting in 1080i – this is fine at the moment for quick live show recording) and two stands in addition to our iPhones. Before our performance, we find the best spots to place the cameras, or we find people (professionals or fans) to film us. This practice has given us a treasure trove of live performances to post on social media, Youtube, or to add to our EPK and website. You never know what kind of performance you are going to have, so the more video you have to choose from, the better. Sometimes the venues have their own video setup or a crew that films on their own. They will often give this footage to you for free or for a nominal fee. If you know how to use editing software, you can edit several performances together and create an even more impactful video by letting the booker see the breadth of your touring.

If the venue has a good sound system and sound crew, the stereo audio captured off of the camera can be very good. However, this is often something that is out of your control. That is why the more video you shoot, the better your odds are at getting something usable. Sometimes, recording with a small digital recorder like the Zoom H1N or the Tascam DR-05x is an excellent way to go. You can place the recorder in a location that is perhaps more optimal for audio than the camera placement, so you'll get better audio results. If you DO rely on the audio from a camera, know that the microphones on most prosumer (entry or midlevel video recorders) are not optimized for all sound, and certainly not from the sheer volume often coming from a stage. An onboard mic upgrade for your camera, or similar for your smartphone, might be required. Good candidates are the Shure MV-88 or Blue Microphone's Snowball (with USB-to-Lightning cable for connection).

Getting a multitrack audio recording of your performance is often the best option. You can take these tracks and put them in Protools, Digital Performer, Logic, or other sound editing software to create a better mix. This gives you the ability to create a more pro-sounding mix of your performance and lay that under the video. And often (if there is not too much bleed), you can also fix any mistakes that you may have made. Also, if you don't like the sound you got on your instrument that night, you may (again depending on mic bleed from your instrument into the other mics) have the ability to fix your performance.

A short note on the above: Some folks will say that your audio should be absolutely live, that however you sound on a given night, that's what you should present, that you should not overdub or fix live multitrack recordings. We don't agree. You want to (a) put your BEST foot forward, and if you do re-record something, (b) make sure you can back that up and sing or play just as well as that "fixed" recording at your next gig. Together with producer Teo Macero, Miles Davis picked the best takes and best segments from some of his beloved 60's and 70's work, and that's what was released. Frank Zappa would sometimes use live recordings, overdub new vocals or guitar recordings and release those. When trying to get a live video together for promotion, you need to do what it takes to get the best representation of you that you can make within the limits of know-how and budget. On the other hand, don't overdub a tuba when there is clearly not one onstage. No tuba hatred, just friendly advice.

Some venues can make a multitrack recording of your performance off of the soundboard, so make sure to ask. This is all the more common with today's digital soundboards – these options were not so widely available even ten years ago. We always travel with several USB sticks as well as other external drives. That way, the soundperson can give us a multitrack recording of our performance right after the show. Other times they will email it to us sometime after the show or even weeks later. The point is you won't know that this is available to you if you don't ask. All this might seem like a lot to think of while you're getting ready for your show and possibly navigating a tour, and IT IS! But this is the business, and you want to take advantage of every opportunity. You can then take this multitrack and mix it yourself, or go to a friendly engineer and have them generate great-sounding mixes for you, whether to edit into a video or release on streaming platforms. Finally, beware soundboard stereo recordings offered for a price. If the recording only represents what's in the soundboard, then you may be missing bass or drums, and just get a passable recording of your voice and maybe one guitar. Unless you trust the soundperson, don't pay for one of these recordings just yet.

At the very least, a decent video can show you how your show is, how you sound, and where there might be areas for improvement. Our band Incendio benefited so much in the early days from watching our taped shows and making improvements.

BAND PICTURE

Your band picture needs to capture the essence of the group. You will be sending the photo to presenters. It will be on your website and your social media pages. It's what presenter, publicists, and you will send to the press. It's what will represent you in concert programs and fliers, so make sure you like the picture and that it represents you well.

Your picture is often the first thing a presenter will see - sometimes before they see a live clip - so you want it to be impactful.

You will then need to make a high and low-resolution version of your best photo or photos. Usually, a high-resolution version at 300dpi will be used for print reviews and ads, and the low resolution can be used for social media as well as for uploading to sites that maintain size restrictions on uploadable media. Both versions should be kept on your website in the media section so they can be easily downloaded by presenters or whoever may need access to them.

If there has been a change in band members, try to get a new photo that reflects that. It's not always necessary, but sometimes it can become a small issue when your band arrives at a familiar venue and you have a different bandmember, but the only visible promo shows the old bandmember. If Cindy is now on bass, but Sergio is still in the band photo, she might not be too happy about that, especially after driving 6 hours to the venue. Remember to send out the latest and greatest! And give Sergio back his PA system, he's getting upset.

If you have taken new photos, remember to change them out on your media page and let the presenters know. Email them your new photo and remind them to use it in any new promo for the group. Often despite your best efforts, old photos will still make their way into new press releases and promo material. So try to stay on top of any changes - this will increase your chances of all parties using your new photo. It will also keep any new band members happy and feeling appreciated.

STAGE PLOT

The included diagram of a stage plot shows you what you will need to make and send out to the venues. A PDF downloadable file will also live on your media page. This will allow anyone who needs immediate access to your stage plots the ability to go and get them.

So you may be asking, "why is a stage plot so important?" I can tell the sound crew what we need long before we get there.

Your stage plot allows the sound crew to be prepared before you get there. The stage plot lets the sound crew know how many band members there are, how many DI's and mics you need, what side the bass player is going to be on, and everything else about the band's audio needs. Remember that the sound crew is working with many different groups every week or even every night. If you are performing at a festival, you may be one of five to ten bands performing on that stage in one day. The sound crew has to get each group up and performing on time. The more information they have about your needs ahead of your arrival, the easier it will be for them to make you sound great!

Please remember some crucial facts. First, the sound crew is not only dealing with the known variables, but they have to deal with the unforeseen problems of cables breaking, power going out, and amps suddenly not working. Having an accurate and easy-to-read stage plot (or stage plots if you have multi-band configurations) will help things run more smoothly for you upon your arrival and show the crew and presenter that you are a pro. It will show them that you respect them and care about your sound. This goes to the second point: the sound crew holds the audio quality of your presentation in their hands. Don't unnecessarily piss them off or make more work for them. The more clearly and succinctly

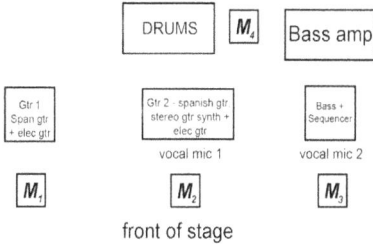

INCENDIO FOUR-PIECE STAGE PLOT 2020 M = monitor

| DRUMS | M_4 | Bass amp |

| Gtr 1
Span gtr
+ elec gtr | Gtr 2 - spanish gtr.
stereo gtr synth +
elec gtr | Bass +
Sequencer |

vocal mic 1   vocal mic 2

M_1 M_2 M_3

front of stage

INCENDIO STAGE INFO

We are a four-piece instrumental group: two guitars, bass, and drums.

WE DO CARRY OUR OWN DI'S.. Our setup is:
1 - Jim (blonde guy): spanish guitar DI
2 - Jim (blonde guy): electric guitar DI
3 - JP (black-haired guy): spanish guitar DI
4 - JP (black-haired guy): electric guitar DI
5 - JP (black-haired guy): guitar synth DI left
6 - JP (black-haired guy): guitar synth DI right
7 - Liza (female): computer/sequencer DI left
8 - Liza (female): computer/sequencer DI right
9 - Liza (female): bass (DI provided)

Drums: 1 kick mic, 2 snare mics (top/bottom), 2 overhead mics,1 hi tom mic, 1 mid tom mic, 1 lo tom mic, 1 hat mic. For smaller rooms, AT LEAST kick, overhead (and hi hat to put in the monitor)

- We need electricity at each of the three guitar locations, the drums, the bass, and sequencer location (near bass) to plug in effects. There needs to be a power strip (or availability of 2-4 plugs) at each electrical station.
- IMPORTANT: We will need a drum rug.

Please check next page for mix notes and monitor recommendations.

Contact JP at

Figure 1 – Incendio 2020 stage plot

detailed your stage plot is, the smoother your show will go. And that's the goal to keep in mind.

An excellent program for generating a basic stage plot with graphics is StagePlotPro, which can be purchased at stageplot.com. At the time of this writing (April 2020), the cost is $39.99.

BAND BIO

A band bio is your story. It lets people know who you are, what you've done, and where you come from. The more interesting you make your bio, the more engaged the reader will be in you and your music. Everyone has a story, and it's up to you to frame it in a creative way that will attract your audience. You don't want to rattle off statistics like a laundry list, but rather frame your accomplishments in a story. Keep in mind that this bio - your story - is going to be in press releases, as well as used in interviews and programs. It will be used in reviews of your shows and your albums. Sometimes people reviewing new material will only restate your written bio, so make sure that it represents you well!

Individual band member bios are also attractive to fans and presenters. If someone in your band has toured with someone of note, or written music for a show, put it in their bio. Perhaps they have done some community outreach or have talents in other areas. Any of these aspects add to the overall story of your group.

I have heard some skeptics say that no one ever reads your bios, but that is not true. I have had fans that I know well, and others that I have met only once, ask me about specifics that they have read on my personal bio and band bio. We have had presenters hire us because they were familiar with one of us from gigs we'd done with other musicians, or from music that we'd written. Had we not included this information in our bio, they would have never known this obscure fact. That small point may have been the one thing that caused them to take a good look at the group and possibly the reason that they gave us a shot. As a musician, you are trying to stand out and get people to listen. Do not disregard your past accomplishments. Use them as part of your story.

I often hear musicians say that they don't want to brag. Bragging and merely stating what you have done previously in your field are two very different things. I guarantee you that no banker goes in for an interview for a new job and doesn't mention their past job experience because they don't want to brag.

PRESS / WRITE-UP

If you have any reviews or press write-ups, keep track of them. You can have a separate tab on your website just for reviews. Include some quotes in your EPK. Use quotes from different write-ups on your promo material or banners. You can even include them on business cards or on the front page of your various social media platforms. Write-ups let people know that you've been around, and others are paying attention.

Whether it's a concert review or someone reviewing your newly recorded release, it's significant to your story.

When you are touring, make sure to check the local papers and ask the presenters if there have been any write-ups on the event or your group. Often they are aware of press releases or articles written about the event but forget to mention it to the artists because they are just so busy. It doesn't hurt to ask. There may be some great reviews sitting out there that would be nice to have up on your website, but you just have not seen it yet. If you are a new group and don't have any reviews as of yet, don't worry, they will come!

WEBSITE

Your website is a holding place for everything about the group. It's a place where the presenter can go and see links to your videos, hear your music, read your bio/bios, read reviews about the group, go to your media page, and download your photos, bios, and stage plot. It's where people can join your mailing list and access any blogs you may be posting. It's a place with links to all of your social media and your EPK. If you are touring and someone needs a picture or stage plot, you can immediately send them to your website, and they can download what they need. You want to make it visually engaging and easy to navigate.

It used to be that the website was the one principal place where a fan or promoter could get all the information they needed. And indeed, there are many resources for making a great website, now more than ever. Artists don't have to learn HTML; they can use sites that offer easy-to-use templates like Wordpress or Wix. Also, a presence on social media is a requirement now. You need to learn how to navigate Facebook, Instagram, and Twitter to reach your audience regularly and tell them what you are up to. It's now a fundamental part of the self-promotion juggernaut, as much as the website itself. A younger demographic might have you gravitating to Snapchat and Instagram more so than Facebook. You can then experiment to find the "sweet spot" for posting daily and weekly content on each platform to keep the range of your audience engaged.

Finally, your website should include all buttons to your social media platforms (Facebook et al), and those social platforms should try to drive traffic back to your website to create a back-and-forth engagement.

EPK

The EPK is a one-page file that has a picture of the group, links to videos, performance highlights, a few reviews or quotes, and links to your social media. That single page has all the pertinent info condensed. The EPK is essentially a small website that allows the promoter to navigate via clickable graphic images (like clickable band photos or still shots) to various landing pages, such as artist website, videos, mp3's, or other content specifically crafted to cater to a promoter's needs. Again, the content on these pages is not necessarily the same content you would share with fans. Rather, it is designed to capture the interest of a promoter and make it easier for them to evaluate you for booking. Now, you CAN make an EPK on your own. But if you are not computer-savvy or don't have the time, you should strongly consider paying a professional to make one for you. We work together with our webmaster, Mark Barnwell (info@markbarnwell.co.uk), to create and update our current EPK.

When you send the EPK via email, start with a short message with a greeting to the promoter, identifying yourself or the band. You should mention the venue and, if possible, how your tour coincides with their location. If not on tour and the venue is regional to your area, indicate your proximity to the gig. A brief mention of previous shows in the area helps too, to show the promoter that you have a regional audience. Then you copy your EPK and paste it in after your brief message to the promoter. Put a picture at the top of the EPK for sure - that way, they see the group picture right away. Take the time to make the EPK engaging. The promoter should have the opportunity to do a short scroll down to all your video links, reviews, and concert highlights. You want your music to be an easy click away, and your reviews and past concerts easily visible to catch their attention.

Your EPK should also live on your website, so you can direct promoters there if you are on the road or otherwise unable to send an email. This can help tremendously, especially in time-sensitive situations.

Note: many online sites offer further support on making an EPK. Some of these sites are:
bandzoogle.com
reverbnation.com
sonicbids.com
Take some time to browse around at what solutions may work best for your needs.

Philosophical side note:
It's been said that sometimes the only thing that you can control is your attitude.

Although your goal is to put all of these materials together into a coherent presentation so that you can ultimately perform, make sure that you allow yourself time to enjoy the process! Wherever you wind up in your career, it is vital to make each step as enjoyable an experience as possible. You will bring that feeling of joy and excitement into your music, gigs, and life. The people that you deal with professionally, whether they be other musicians, show bookers, or your fans, will feel and react to the attitude that you bring with you to every event. If you approach everything besides the final result as a difficult task that you would rather not be doing, it's going to be a hard and unpleasant road, and it's going to show. Each one of the tasks we have mentioned is creative in its own right, whether it's getting a band picture, writing a bio, or putting together a contract. You will learn things about yourself and your other band members. You will make mistakes so prepare to

INCENDIO

Incendio Band website	Youtube

Incendio Latin/World music experience

Our four-piece group can expand to an eight-piece with violin, percussion, B3 organ and dancer - or break down to a guitar duo and anything in between.

Incendio presents a show with fiery rhythms, memorable melodies, and a spell-binding performance. They are also available for educational workshops.

Incendio has trailblazed their own path since 2000 with 11 CDs, Billboard chartings, extensive international touring and over eighty million Pandora spins.

Incendio is:

Jean-Pierre Durand	- Guitar and Guitar Synth
Jim Stubblefield	- Guitar
Liza Carbe	- Bass
Tim Curle	- Drums

Guest Musicians:

Aubrey Richmond	- Violin
Arleen Hurtado	- Dance
Al Velasquez	- Percussion
Carey Frank	- B3 Organ

Azucar

Capetown Juerga

Mitra's Dance

Eyes of the World

CONCERT HIGHLIGHTS

National Gallery of Art, Washington DC 6x
Belshan World Music Festival, China
Islands Folk Festival, British Columbia 2x
Clayton Opera House, NY
Redlands Bowl, CA
California Worldfest, Grass Valley, CA
Jazz in the Park, Milwaukee, WI 2x
Musikfest, Bethlehem PA 5x
Strawberry Music Festival, Northern CA 4x
Chico World Music Festival, CA
Phoenix World Festival, AZ
Desert Botanical Garden, Phoenix AZ 4x
Tempe Performing Arts Center, AZ
Rhythm and Roots Concerts, Tucson AZ 5x
San Antonio Jazz Festival, TX
Floydfest, Floyd VA
Temecula Theater, CA
Millpond Music Festival, Bishop, CA
The Hult Center, Eugene, OR with Ballet Fantastique
Redwood Jazz Festival, Eureka, CA 3x
Spencer Theater, Ruidoso, New Mexico
Spaghettini Jazz and Supper Club, Seal Beach, CA
Oxnard Performing Arts Center, CA
Catamount Concerts, St. Johnsbury, VT

Clark Museum, Williamstown, MA
NedFest, Nederland, CO
Salem World Music Festival, OR
Mauch Chunk Opera House, Jim Thorpe, PA 5x
Tanner Amphitheater, Springdale, Utah 4x
Levitt Steelstacks, Bethlehem, PA
Levitt Pavilion, Pasadena, CA 6x
Levitt Pavilion, Los Angeles, CA 2x
Levitt Pavilion, Westport, CT 5x
Levitt Pavilion, Memphis, TN 2x
Levitt Pavilion, Arlington, TX, CA 2x
Allegretto Vineyard, Paso Robles, CA
Verizon Jazz Concerts, Pasadena, CA
Indian Wells Art Festival, Indian Wells, CA 11x
Catalina Jazz Tracks, Catalina Island, CA 2x
Catalina's Jazz Club, Hollywood, CA
Midvale UT Summer Concerts
Lucca Winery, Modesto, CA
Empire State Summer Noon Concerts, Albany, NY
Lake George Summer Concerts, NY
Reston Town Center, VA 5x
Levitt AMP Series, Carson City, CA
Gardens of the World, Thousand Oaks, CA
The Triple Door, Seattle, WA

Figure 2 – Incendio EPK

30

laugh at yourself and try again. It's a learning process, so have fun.

Maybe you feel that there are trying moments that you would love to move beyond and reach that next level. If you stay the course and complete some of these steps, you may find yourself reflecting on mistakes or bad situations in a more positive light. You may also find that some of those difficult times were blessings in disguise. Allow yourself to enjoy the moment, for it will not come again.

Chapter 2
Production – making YOUR music

The reality is that many of you are simply not interested in learning the technical aspects of recording and producing, and that's fine. It's a complete skill on its own and certainly not one that can be explained in one chapter of a book. If you want someone to help you, you'll need to find a producer. If not, you can and should learn to do it yourself.

In all cases, you should familiarize yourself with some of the processes involved in producing music – how to record, which microphones to use, etc. If you don't have the slightest idea of how things work, it can be frustrating trying to convey your ideas. You can also get frustrated with your producer when things aren't sounding the way you want them to right away.

Let's first talk about finding the right producer for your project. You want to get someone who is a good producer, but you also need someone that you like and with whom you have a good rapport. Just because someone won a Grammy or produced someone that you love does not mean that she or he will be a good fit for you. There have been many artists that have been VERY unhappy after choosing a producer solely for those reasons which we previously mentioned. If you have a contentious relationship with your producer, the whole process is going to be very stressful and upsetting. If that producer decides not to listen to any of your ideas, you are going to be very unhappy. If that producer doesn't capture the essence of your music or you as an artist, it can be heartbreaking. Don't be blinded by things that might not benefit you and your music in the long run.

Years ago when there were still development deals, the label would give the artist money to go in and record several songs or even an album. Often someone at the label would hire a producer or engineer friend to produce the project so they could get the money. That producer or engineer was often the completely wrong person for the artist. In the end it was a lost opportunity for the artist, which left them heartbroken and disillusioned. Today, artists are more in control of their destiny and have the opportunity to choose a producer. Take that power and use it wisely. Don't be intimidated or seduced by credentials.

Consider doing one or two songs with a producer to see how you work together, what they bring to the table, and how responsive they are to your suggestions. If they do not agree with you, ask them to explain why. They may have some very good reasons for not doing it your way that in time might seem better to you. But if it looks like you will just butt heads, then you're only out the money for one or two produced songs instead of a whole album.

Understanding the process is very important. Familiarize yourself with basics. The following are a couple of thoughts on how to move forward.

If you are a solo musician and you're going to come in

with your guitar or piano, and that's it, then fine. You're going to be concerned about the usual stuff while recording: what best microphone and mic preamp best captures your voice, and the same for the instrument you are playing. But if you're not coming in as a self-contained solo artist, you either have a band or need to get one for your recording and your live shows. There are a lot of professional studio musicians who mostly record – if they go out for shows, they will usually be compensated quite a bit more than your budget can afford for a beginning touring artist. But you'll want their expertise and know-how to best record your song. Ideally, this is a conversation between you and your producer. If your producer is seasoned and has been around a while, he or she should have no trouble proposing a variety of drummers, bassists, keyboardists, guitarists, backing vocalists. Chances are that this producer has a history with these folks and knows how to get the best out of them for your production. Now, sometimes even if they give their best performance, you might feel they are missing the point of what you are trying to produce – maybe they are playing too hard, not playing hard enough, maybe they are right on the beat when perhaps they should be slightly ahead of the beat or slightly behind the beat (which could be the topic of entirely different book). In this case, it is again essential to have a good dialogue with your producer on how you think the player might approach the song differently if they are not getting it right. The best studio musicians will always listen to the artist and producer – they WANT to get it right for you.

Now, if you are a band, know that when those microphones are put in place, they will reveal how much you've practiced and what your strengths are. They will also reveal any weaknesses or inconsistencies in your playing. Rehearse well before you record. Try playing to click track to see if you can keep some semblance of good time going. Now, not all bands record to a click, and a little amount of movement can add to the swing or excitement of a track. But more often than not, we have found that the artists arguing most against this approach are the ones who have trouble staying in time – it's a simple fact that keeps repeating itself over and over. Walk in having practiced, be humble, and be open to constructive criticism. If the producer or fellow artists are being jerks, that's a different problem! If that happens, you have to be ready to defend your approach firmly, but hopefully not in anger – most of the time, anger will undermine the point you are trying to make. Remember that the goal is to create a great track and be prepared to do what it takes to fulfill that artistic responsibility.

JP and I are big believers in pre-production. We would like to hear the songs, perhaps prep some demos, and provide a polished final product. Pre-production is the process of going through the songs with the artist and deciding on an approach. Maybe the producer thinks that something you heard as a more acoustic-type ballad might be better expressed as a raging rock song or vice versa. Ultimately it's your call, but usually, the best product comes from an artist and a producer who are in lockstep, who have the same vision of the artists' material. In the case of

Incendio (and most of our productions in general), we demo out songs as does our partner Jim Stubblefield, putting down bass, guitar, keys and drums with a click track provided by a DAW (desktop audio workshop) like Protools, Logic, or in our case, Digital Performer. Once that rough is in place, and we like the feel, we send this to one of the drummers with whom we regularly play (in the case of Incendio, our drummer Timothy Curle who "grooves" particularly well to a click track). They lay down the fundamental groove, and we build the track around that, usually replacing our rough tracks with new "keeper" tracks that are even more grooving and locked to the drums.

Know that if the drummer is not solid, it will compromise your whole project. You might not know what is off, but everyone will feel it. Nothing will ever sit right because there is not a solid foundation for everyone else to lock to. So make sure you at least record with a great drummer. A producer or engineer can go in and edit and beat correct. It happens all the time, but it will cost you time and money for your producer to do that work instead of getting it right the first time. If you can get a solid drummer from the outset, you'll get better, more grooving results.

Of course, there are also productions where we simply record a band playing all together, no click, just listening to each other. This approach always works better if the band has played a lot together and knows the song reasonably well. These kinds of sessions can yield a lively track. But they take preparation and a studio that can accommodate everyone playing and being able to see each other at the same time for subtle head nods, eye contact to keep things locked, etc.

This leads to an important point that I'll let JP explain. "When I was in high school, I read an article in the late, great Musician magazine that made a profound impact on me. I read an interview with producer Bill Laswell, who strongly made the point that a record is a moment in time, a reflection of where you are now. Sometimes it's the best you can do, sometimes not, but it is a representation of you NOW. If you continue to fulfill your artistic mission, there will be more shows, more recordings, and more time spent on your craft. As we said earlier in the book, just move forward. Don't re-record your album three times! Put it out there and keep on moving."

Also, remember that the process takes as long as it takes, within reason. We have had clients that come in and expect to have a quality recording ready in a few hours, or two days. But the more work required of the producer to form what the artists want, and the longer it takes to record satisfactory instrumental parts and vocals, the longer the process will take. In short, if you want something great, it takes time. This is particularly true for newer artists, and without knowing the process, they can be amongst the most impatient.

Another critical point: if I had a dime for every artist that told me that "their producer has the masters and I can't get them back," we'd have, well, a massive stack o' dimes! It is well within your rights to ask your producer for a backup of the files since you are paying for the sessions. Buy your own inexpensive hard drive, maybe 500 gigabytes or a terabyte. Let the producer/engineer know that you'd like to back up your sessions. This process will protect you if something happens to your producer, or there is a breakdown in communications, and the producer holds the tracks hostage. If this is because you are not paying them, shame on you. But if it is for another reason either out of their or your control, at least you have some of your work.

Understand that a rough mix is just that. It's not finished! If you are recording guitars and the drums are turned up, perhaps it's because the guitarist or producer wants them to help the guitarist lock to while she is recording. If the producer is working on a synth part, it's possibly very loud in the mix because it a work in progress. If one part is muted because the person recording their part only wants to hear certain instruments, keep in mind that those parts can and most likely will be reintroduced when it comes time to mix. So the point is you don't need to continually ask why some part is so loud or why it's not there. When everything thing is recorded and the mixing begins, that is the time to start addressing those considerations. Before mixing, take notes of the parts you feel that are missing, so you can double-check to put them back in at mix time.

A lot of artists don't understand the importance of mastering. Mastering can make or break all the hard work you have done to this point. Mastering is a very specialized process, where your mastering person takes the stereo tracks of the mix you've made and puts them into their mastering system. When done right, the process will ensure that your music sounds the best on the widest variety of playback mediums. The bass won't be boomy, the highs won't be too strident, and the mids will sound full and not harsh. If your producer has taken care to make sure these components were recorded and mixed well, then you can give the mastering engineer a product that they can improve even more. If your final recordings are compromised and don't sound that great, there is only so much "fixing" that the mastering engineer can do. These days, there are a lot of folks advertising that they do mastering. Some put your music through some of the same basic software that you can get off the shelf. They claim reasonably low prices and possibly don't do much work on your track – they just limit the track for maximum loudness, add some bass for foundation, and 10 minutes and a few hundred bucks later, they hand you back your song. Other "more legit" mastering houses pride themselves on one signal path (usually one expensive EQ and one expensive compressor), and that's "their" sound, which is great unless you don't want "their" sound. You want to look for someone with experience who also charges a reasonable amount, but will hand you the best finished product. Time and time again, we have gone to our friends at Becker Mastering. They do a great job and have a great attitude, and will work on everything from us (Spanish guitar) to Neil Diamond to Macklemore!

http://www.beckermastering.com

PRODUCING YOURSELF

First off, all of the advice above also applies to producing yourself. Time is still always money. You must be able to clearly convey to your band or studio musicians how to play their parts to fulfill your vision. Learning how to describe your musical desires takes time. Going to school to learn is never a bad idea, whether it's a college, Musicians Institute, or a program at a recording studio school like Full Sail. There are also enough tutorials on Youtube to demystify some of the processes that took us years to learn.

Be patient. One of the best things you can do is just start recording. Look online to see which mics are used for certain types of voices, or for which guitars, or for which piano. See which recording platform makes the most sense to you. Often folks just start by committing to one system and learning it – if you do this, it won't take long to learn a different system since they all mostly complete the same function. Those programs, or DAW's, include Pro Tools, Digital Performer, Logic Pro, Cubase, and Reaper, among many others.

One way to distinguish these a little bit is simple: Pro Tools was one of the first and most robust audio recording platforms. By contrast, programs like Performer and Logic Pro (and Opcode Vision and a few other back in the day) were developed primarily as sequencers to control synthesizer programs. Pro Tools is the industry standard for movies and TV, but it HAD to add sequencer functionality to be able to do the processes that Performer and Logic were doing. Conversely, Digital Performer and Logic added the audio recording functionality because they had to. So generally, Pro Tools is better at controlling audio and not quite as good at sequencing, and Digital Performer and Logic are better at controlling sequences and less good at manipulating audio. However, that gap has gotten much, much smaller over the last few years, with producer workflows with audio and sequences moving quickly on all platforms. All of these platforms have made a move towards making it a little more affordable for you to jump in. GarageBand by Apple is a particularly useful "starter" platform to prepare you for using Logic, and for learning about this world in general.

As we stated earlier, there are many books written on how to produce. We're going to give you just a taste of some industry terms and tips, primarily for the beginner, or the intermediately trained musician who wants to jump into the recording game.

In the most basic setup, you're going to need three items: a computer, an interface, and a microphone. For a computer, you can run most if not all of the main DAW programs on a Mac or a PC. We are Mac people and think that it's a pretty sturdy system on which to run your music studio. You have to jump through a few more hoops to make your PC run these different software programs, but it's not too bad, mainly since it usually costs a little less to purchase a PC than to buy a Mac. For the beginner, a two or three-year-old Mac laptop, an iMac, or a Mac mini (with additional inexpensive monitor) might be a cost-effective solution.

Next, you're going to need some sort of audio interface. You will be plugging your microphone and your guitar, bass, or keyboard into this unit. The unit then connects to the computer - usually via USB, FireWire, or Thunderbolt – allowing recording on the DAW in your computer. In almost all cases, better interfaces are usually amongst the most expensive. You do get what you pay for. MOTU (Mark of the Unicorn), who also make the DAW Digital Performer, make some very good interfaces and basic two-channel interfaces – there's a lot of bang for the buck there. But you could also check out two-channel offerings from Focusrite, Presonus, RME, Apogee, Apollo, and so many more. If you are just starting out, there are several models you can find that are in the $200 to $300 range that should work fine to start. There are super-cheap ones too, but those don't offer great audio quality. Even worse, they may only be limitedly compatible with your system, especially if they are older. Buyer beware.

Finally, you are going to need a microphone. There are two kinds of mics you'll be comparing initially: dynamic and condenser. Dynamic mics like the Shure 57 and 58 are found regularly on stages and studios around the world. These are basic microphones that will get the job done, and are usually in the $100 and below range. If you want something that sounds better, you can pay a little more for condenser microphones. These are built differently and usually get a better sound – you'll tend to see less of these on stage, more often finding them in the studio. These require phantom power, which is a switch that you should find on any decent audio interface. Your vocal and your acoustic guitar will probably sound better using these mics. Your electric guitar, on the other hand, will probably overpower a condenser mic if you are micing an amp and not using amp emulation software. So if you plan to record a lot of electric guitar with an amp, initially, it's probably best to get a Shure SM57 dynamic mic. You can also use this for vocals to begin with. Experiment to see what kinds of sounds you can get. Singing from far away will sound very different than singing close.

At this point, it's best to say there are many aspects of production, and there is a lot of valuable information available online. I would suggest that you watch some educational videos from different producers on mic technique, the different types of mics, micing an amp, and micing your vocal. The more fluent you are in the terminology used, the easier it will be to communicate and get your ideas across.

Philosophical side note:
Say yes, and then figure out.

When JP and I started working together in 1995, it was kind of a perfect storm. I had a lot of midi equipment, a soundboard, and some mics. I was making recordings, but I had a lot to learn. All the wiring and signal chain knowledge did not come easily or naturally. Conversely, JP loved to wire things up and get them going but didn't have a lot of equipment of his own. Both of us knew that if we wanted to make our living in music, we would have to learn a lot about production, recording, and engineering ourselves. We were offered an opportunity to write music for "Entertainment Tonight," and when that happened, we said "yes"! We didn't know what music we would do, and we didn't have much of a studio to complete the task. But sometimes, when you say "yes," you will find a way to do it, and that's what we did! Those several hundreds of minutes we wrote in many different styles became the foundation of our writing career. We read recording books, had friends help us, and took work where we "learned on the job," doing paid and non-paid projects where we learned our craft. We tried new techniques, we learned about EQ, reverb, and compression and tried to learn how to apply those to our mixes best. There was a lot of trial and error, but we stuck to our guns. We also didn't BS our clients – we did not charge them for learning on the job, only for the work we did for them directly. If you behave ethically with your clients, they will either come back or refer you to others, or you'll get to keep a friendship with them at the very least. If you go in trying to work every angle to your benefit, that represents the least desirable elements of the music industry, and your bad reputation will precede you. If someone is spreading lies about you, usually the truth will come out in time.

In short, seize the means of production. Learn to do it all yourself, or at least familiarize yourself with every aspect. Make sure to treat your clients and musicians with respect. This will establish longevity and trust; you will come to appreciate the fruits of your labor many years down the road!

Check out "Modern Recording Techniques" by David Huber as a reference book on techniques. This is one of many helpful texts available.

Chapter 3
Booking - Finding the Venues

• Identify your audience
• Festival, theater, and club databases
• Booking conferences - what they are and how to maximize your visit.
• Organization of contacts
• The actual booking process

First and foremost: identify your audience!

You have to identify your audience before you do anything. Then you can always start looking for local gigs in the entertainment section of your local newspaper. Then go ahead and do this same check on the regional level. You will probably find that you can do some of this information gathering yourself, but you'll also find it's hard to collect this information quickly and effectively. This chapter will help you explore your options.

As you expand your booking horizons, you should take a good look at what kind of act you are and how and where that might fit. Are you a cover band, and if so, what genre? Are you a tribute band? Do you do original singer-songwriter material? Do you perform original rock songs? Do you play electronic dance music?

One of the first places to start finding venues to perform - beyond your local venues - are festival, theater, and club databases. There are many different databases, each one having a unique set of parameters, often focusing on one type of venue more than another. Websites include Festivalnet.com, Pollstar.com, and Concertsinyourhome.com, amongst others.

Another suitable place to look at are booking conferences like WAA (Western Arts Alliance), and many more that will be discussed in detail shortly. These are the places to start. Understanding how to best use these databases and conferences will determine how successful you will be in getting gigs.

DATABASES

Once you have a venue in mind, one of the most challenging and time-consuming processes you'll have to undertake is finding the correct contact person. All the education and rehearsal you have done cannot prepare you for the tedium of trying to ferret out the right person with whom you need to speak. You wanted to play music professionally, and all of a sudden, you've become a private investigator! Access to a variety of databases to find the right contacts (along with many other reasons that will become obvious) is crucial. They provide all the necessary information to start your quest. There have been databases over the years that provided these contacts, but you needed to track them down, which wasn't as easy or cost-effective as it is now. They have become easier to find and much more affordable. There are a variety of online databases that give you venues, festivals, cultural arts centers, clubs, house concerts, fairs, and just about any potential venue for which you are searching. You do have to pay, but it's not much and well worth it. Like purchasing a good instrument, these fees will pay for themselves after a time. Amongst our favorites are:

http://www.festivalnet.com - This site covers festivals, fairs, art festivals, and the like. They do NOT typically include clubs or theaters. The cost to become a member ranges from $49/$59/$89 per year, with different features at each level.

https://www.pollstar.com/pollstarpro is now a subscription service at $598 a year. Individual digital lists, such as "Record Labels," "Concert Support Services," "Booking Agents," "Talent Buyers," "Major Concert Venues," "Colleges, Fairs, Festivals, Theme Parks," and "Artist Management" are available for $499.99 each.

Although the layout of each database may vary, the ones we are familiar with all contain the necessary information that is needed to contact the presenter (or at least the main office) and get your EPK out to them. Many allow you to search by location, the type of entertainment (or if they even HAVE feature entertainment – many festivals don't, but many DO), the style of music, time of year, and how many people will be attending, amongst other parameters.

We have been using several different ones over the years. These are always growing and changing, so try to be aware of new databases that are springing up. Some examples are:

- http://www.indieonthemove.com
- http://www.gigmor.com
- http://www.gigsalad.com
- http://www.sonicbids.com
- http://www.festivalfinder.com
- http://www.festivals.com
- http://www.musicfestivalwizard.com
- http://www.jambase.com
- http://www.fairsandfestivals.net
- http://www.bandsurfing.com

Pollstar has venues big and small. You can find festivals, clubs, and all sorts of venues that book live music. Pollstar is more expensive than just about all the other platforms, but it also has a far bigger database and longer history. This may or may not be useful to you. You can narrow your search by plugging in how big of a venue you are looking for and the type of venue, be it a festival, club, or something else. They provide you with the name and contact information of the person who is in charge of booking. It will have a link to the website, so you can get a look at the venue, a list of who has performed there in the past, and similar info. If you are looking at a festival or art show, you can see how many people they expect to be attending.

With all that information, it is now up to you to send that email, make that call and do your best to ingratiate yourself with that contact person so you can at least get a shot at a booking.

After a few years, we found our band to be a better fit

for festivals than clubs. Thus, festivalnet.com has been an essential website for us. It does not contain clubs, so the list of potential shows is a little easier to digest. I'd say that it is super-important to get into a few festivals early on, even small ones, and then use that to build your "resume." If a festival sees you have already done a few, you are more likely to get booked at a slightly larger festival. The different tiers in Festivalnet.com reflect different levels of functionality of their site (from basic access to being able to save a list of your best prospects, to loading and using an EPK on their website).

In the last 20 years, the notion of playing at and hosting house concerts has exploded. These are audiences of 30-100 or more people at someone's house, simply enjoying the music. There is a cool site called concertsinyourhome.com. This one was put together by a touring musician that created a database of house concerts for himself, and it grew into something he decided to share. It's set up to help musicians find house concerts and to help presenters find musicians. Concerts in Your Home encourages you to reach out to venues as well as giving you a platform to put up a profile of your group that includes videos, audio clips, and information about the group so that venues can find you.

You can book a tour of just house concerts or combine them with other venues. People sponsoring house concerts sometimes provide rooms for the musicians to spend the night – sometimes they also offer meals. Some house concerts provide food or snacks for the guests, and some are set up like a potluck with all the guests contributing to the event. Fans still buy albums and t-shirts to help support the artists.

House concerts can be an excellent and supportive environment for musicians. People are there because they are music lovers - they are there to hear your music and your stories. They like to be able to interact and socialize with the musicians. It's all part of the charm of house concerts. It's an intimate environment for the musicians and the patrons. It does tend to work better for solo artists, duos, or smaller-sized ensembles.

The sponsors of the concerts, who are the people that live in the house where you will be performing, charge an entrance fee - usually, all or most of the money goes to the artist. Sometimes the person who is sponsoring the concert will take out a nominal amount to cover their expenses. It's a great way to get new fans and make money in the process. As you start playing house concerts, you will find out about other house concerts from the people that booked you or from other patrons.

There are house concerts all over the world, and becoming part of Concerts in Your Home is a good way to familiarize yourself with the culture and get plugged in.

BOOKING CONFERENCES

A few times a year, the most important national and regional venues go hunting for acts to perform at their theaters, clubs, and festivals. And often the most prominent agents - CAA, Columbia Artists, Paradigm, Ted Kurland Presents, Cadence Arts Network, and the like – come out to present artists to those venues.

These are some of the main annual booking conferences in the United States. APAP is the biggest and most nationally-oriented of them all in terms of presenters and attendance, with WAA second, followed by some of the others listed here. We didn't find out about the existence and importance of these conferences for about the first 4 or 5 years of our band. As we are primarily self-taught in booking, there was no way to find out UNTIL we got our first agent. We offer this critical PSA: for all these conferences, the registration dates and showcase applications happen LONG before these conference dates, so if they look interesting to you, go immediately to the website and see when you need to apply for a showcase or for rooms – many offer early bird specials on registration so that you can save a bit of money – if it seems appealing, don't wait to do your research!

APAP (Association of Performing Arts Professionals) – New York City, mid-January (Globalfest, which concentrates on global world music, happens in conjunction with this festival)
https://www.apap365.org/Conference

WAA (Western Arts Alliance) – venue varies throughout the Western US, usually end of August or beginning of September
https://www.westarts.org/

Arts Midwest – venue usually varies through the northern Midwest US, early September - https://www.artsmidwest.org

Arts Northwest – venue usually varies through Pacific Northwest, mid-October - https://www.artsnw.org/

PAE (Performing Arts Exchange) presented by South Arts – venue varies, usually through the southeastern US states. This conference has been dissolved as of 2019, but we keep it in this list, so you know what it was and, more importantly, which area it represented. We think something new will spring up here in the next few years.

Folk Alliance – this is an extraordinary set of conferences, insofar as many bookers and agents are there, but this conference concentrates on, you guessed it, folk music. And when we say folk music, we mean all strains: singer/songwriters, world music with a folk bent, loud alt-country groups with an acoustic guitar played by someone wearing leather. In other words, it's not just single guys and gals playing a Martin, and thus, it is a very rich experience. Also, unlike the conferences listed above, the hotels agree to allow artists to showcase in their rooms, sometimes with minimal or no amplification. Walking (or stumbling) from hotel room to hotel room at these events is a unique and wonderful experience, where you can hear some of the most intense and moving artist experiences just a few feet away, shared by no more than the number of people that can fit in a room. If you are an acoustic artist, you

MUST consider the national event at some point.
There are also smaller events that are great, perhaps not quite as impactful as the absolute immersion one receives at the national event, which takes place at the end of January. http://www.folk.org
The regional conferences reach into Canada and Mexico and can be viewed at https://www.folk.org/page/Regions

FAR_West Folk Alliance Region West – from California up through Canada to Alaska – mid-October

SWRFA – Southwest Regional Folk Alliance – from Arizona through Texas including Mexico) – late September

SERFA – Southeast Regional Folk Alliance - including Florida, Mississippi, and the Carolinas) – mid-May

FARM – Folk Alliance Region Midwest - Indiana up through Illinois through central Canada – late October

NERFA – Northeast Regional Folk Alliance – from Maryland through Pennsylvania up through Maine, New Brunswick and eastern Canada) – early November

NACA (National Association of Campus Activities) – this is a conference where universities and colleges send representatives to look at prospective acts for their schools. Magicians, comedians, and hypnotists do well here, as do younger acts that are energetic

songwriters, or hip-hop based musicians that again appeal to a younger crowd. Be ready to do a lot of follow-ups because the representatives the schools send are usually kids themselves, and it can be a bit of a challenge to get a response from a younger person who is also trying to study and do their regular workload. The main conference is February, but they also have several smaller conferences divided by national regions:
https://www.naca.org/

South (Virginia, Mississippi, Florida, etc.)– early October

Central US (Colorado, Oklahoma, Texas, etc.)– early October

Mid Atlantic (New York, Delaware, Maryland, etc.) – mid-October

Mid America (Michigan, Ohio, Illinois, etc.) – late October

Northeast (Maine, Vermont, Quebec, etc.) – early November

West (California, Hawaii, Utah, etc.) – mid-November

Northern Plains (Montana, the Dakotas, Iowa, etc.) – early April

Then, of course, there's South by Southwest in Austin, Texas, or SXSW. It's quite a scene, and a lot of up and coming new bands. But unless you have a buzz, and are willing to spend a fair amount of money to get there and present in a half-way decent slot, you should probably concentrate on the other conferences before you commit to the hugeness of SXSW.

Now, booking conferences are important and very valuable! They are expensive to attend, but you can contact and possibly perform in front of different promoters, bookers, and presenters over a several day period. There are two key components of reaching out to prospective "buyers," who can book you: the showcases, and attending the conference itself. These are two separate and distinct activities.

First, you can apply for an "official" juried showcase, where your act is handpicked to present in the "main event." If you don't get into that or choose not to apply, you can also do the "guerilla" after-hours showcases that often happen on-premises.

Second, you can get a booth at the "marketplace" or the "floor." This is where all the people OFFERING talent (agents, yourself if you are representing your own band) sit and wait for a promoter to walk by your booth, show interest, and engage you in questions about your act: your cost, your availability during specific dates, etc.

Here's the breakdown of these two activities. We will use WAA fees as an example. Important: Arts Midwest and Arts Northwest can be anywhere from 2/3 to 1/2 of the cost of WAA and possibly more effective for you, so you should probably attend one of those first to prepare yourself. APAP and WAA tend to be the most expensive of the regional events. APAP doesn't put on or directly administrate their own main showcases, and the other regionals will charge less.

For most conferences besides APAP, you can apply for a juried showcase – you pay to apply. This fee is not refundable even if you don't get picked for the showcase. These showcases are in one of the main rooms at the conference. The application fee at WAA is $95. If you are selected for the juried showcase, you will pay them $800 for it, minus that $95 application fee. They generally have a nice stage, sound system, and crew to help set everything up and keep the showcases moving along - in other words, they get each act on and off stage quickly, so the program stays on schedule. Your showcase time is usually between 20 to 30 minutes depending on the conference. The juried showcases generally happen earlier in the evening than the "guerilla" showcases and presenters are encouraged strongly to attend – this is the main reason why they can be significant and possibly more useful for band promotion than the guerilla showcases.

Guerilla showcases, or the "after hours" showcases, happen later in the evening in smaller rooms. These showcases last about 15 minutes each.

One person or business entity rents the room and provides the sound system (this could be you – many independent artists host their own showcase room and host a few bands, charging them for the slot to defray the cost). This person is responsible for putting together the schedule of performers and keeping things running on time. As a performer, you have to find who has a guerilla showcase room and contact that person. This type of showcase is often listed on the website of the conference. They will let you know if they have any spots available and how much you have to pay for a spot on their schedule. These 15-minute showcases can run anywhere from $400 to $1000 depending on who is running the room, what they charge, the size of the room, and the size of the PA necessary to convey the best version of your act. Some of these rooms are well-established and do more to promote their showcases than others. This is where your research will come in. You need to reach out to potential guerrilla showcase bookers and try to find out as much as you can about them and the showcase room that they run.

Now to recap: if you have not been invited to the main showcase, you're in about $400-$1000 on a guerilla showcase to start. That's not transporting your band, or paying them if they are simply backing you up. And that's not hotel rooms either. You also need to spend some time promoting your showcase to the attendees. You'd think that this could be in the form of a Facebook ad or Instagram reach out, but the truth is that the most important names, the presenter contacts, are only made available if you register for the event. If an agent represents you, they will have the list and will have paid the full conference fee to attend.

This brings us to the second conference activity –

attendance and being in the "marketplace" or on the "floor." Now, why is registration second in our list, when it seems like attendance would be more fundamentally important? Because you can showcase, either via main or guerilla, without actually attending the conference. However, if you do not have an agent, or someone representing you in the "marketplace," we advise against this. You can't actually showcase without representation of some sort, even if it's self-representation.

So let's say, for the sake of argument, that you, like us, wish to showcase AND represent yourself at the "marketplace," which is usually the restricted "main ballroom" of whatever hotel at which you stay. They will check a badge, and you won't be able to get in otherwise. Let's again use WAA, one we have attended a few times, as an example.

Juried showcase = $800 if you are picked.

Guerilla showcase = $400 to $1000, sometimes even more depending on the size of the presentation – dance troupes, who also attend these conferences, require a large stage or open area in which to dance, hence bigger rooms.

CONFERENCE ATTENDANCE & MEMBERSHIP: There's registration to the conference, and then there's actual year-long membership in WAA. Your regular registration fee for the event is $570 for a WAA member (that's another cost), or $695 for a non-member. You can become a member on a sliding scale. For artists that make under $100,000 a year touring, the cost (as of 2019) is $275 to become a member of WAA officially and thus receive all sorts of non-conference booking and arts information. A good point to know is that for conference registration, there are early-bird specials that knock off a bit of the cost. And, if you want to attend at the last minute on-site at the hotel, it will be a bit more. There are also one-day passes and discount student registration available. There are great workshops available during the day at the conference, on topics like arts funding, self-management, learning how to be a better agent, and so forth.

So now you have a sense of general costs. Since you most likely have not attended before, you will be a newbie and will be the last to be able to register to get a booth. Note: at WAA, if you get a booth, you also get one conference registration rolled into this cost, which takes the sting out a bit. In other words, the person attending the event as an agent on behalf of the band automatically gets to attend the conference. However, this person does need to be a member of WAA, so he or she would have to pay that initial $275 to become a member.

"Booths" start with a small "bistro tabletop." Someone who has been there for years and years will pay $645. You, as a new person, will pay $1,160. That's the sliding scale they have instituted, with longtime agencies getting a break. If you go with a full booth, 8' by 8', and go as a new attendee, you are looking at $1,279.

We have not included:
• Membership dues, which should be $275 for you.
• hotel
• transportation
• the cost of marketing materials: postcards, floor banners, CD's/USB stick with your music, possible ads in the print version or mobile version of the program (the mobile is probably better - we think it gets a little more bang for the buck in this day and age)

For a standard booth (including registration) plus booking yourself or your full band in a guerilla showcase, which is a pretty standard configuration for an indie artist, at WAA, you're fundamentally looking at:

8' by 8' Booth: $1,279
membership: $ 275
One guerilla showcase $ 400
======
Grand total of your first
conference, no frills, no
Hotels, no meals, no
Parking $1,954

So, to get in the game at WAA on the ground floor (with a full booth – you can get a smaller booth or bistro table, but the difference is within about $100) is around $2000.

Now, you add the cost of the band coming and doing the showcase, the cost of the hotel rooms, meals, marketing materials, and the time for reaching out to presenters beforehand to let them know you'll be

Figure 3: Incendio's postcards from WAA 2019
(front is color, back is black and white to keep
costs down – we use http://www.vistaprint.com regularly)

there, and you can understand why so many artists choose NOT to attend. There's a common adage that you "need to attend WAA for three years or more for folks there to possibly take a chance on you, or even to realize you're there." We think that's generally true. There are ways to minimize your outlay, and we'll get to that shortly. If you decide to do this, you MUST personally reach out to presenters and anyone else that you would like to see your showcase and let them know (1) who you are and (2) where and what time you will be performing. If you register on your own, you will be supplied with a database of all attendees, so you need to do your research before you go and reach out to these folks.

This is important: you're going to get a list that might contain 300 to 500 presenters. DON'T MAKE A BLANKET EMAIL AND SEND TO EVERYONE. They will more than likely ignore it. You could be the best thing since sliced cheese (and who doesn't love sliced cheese?), but you're still not going to fit at every venue. If this is your first conference, pick a region or state nearby you and look through the list of available venues. Take the time to look up the venues in your state and look at their roster of events. If you specialize in Celtic-tinged originals, and the venue has booked Celine Dion, they're not going to book you. If the venue has dinner theater including "Oklahoma," "Paint Your Wagon," and "Hair," they probably won't book you. Spend the time to direct your effort to venues that will book you. Also, know that they are seasonal. If you attend WAA in September of 2019, those venues are more than likely booking 2020 and into 2021. It's a long game at these conferences, which is yet another reason why they say you need to attend for a few years. They are essentially trying to make sure that you're for real. Which is an expensive way of continually proving your existence, but it is what it is.

So we would suggest starting with Arts Midwest, Arts Northwest or Folk Alliance. They are smaller, less expensive, and you are more likely to get traction at one of these on your first time out than you are at WAA or APAP.

When you arrive at the conference, there are many different opportunities to meet and socialize with the other attendees, so make sure you come armed with cards or fliers that clearly say where and when you are performing. Vistaprint or Kinko's can be invaluable in this regard, but don't wait until the last minute! You will be able to put these different fliers on tables as well as passing them out. But if they tell you not to put flyers out yet, or go paperless for environmental concerns, LISTEN TO THEM! You can get away with a modest print of 50-100 specialized cards and hand them only to suitable prospects. You should also be ready to hand out 10-30 CD's/USB sticks as calling cards. You will also want to make some floor banners to put up outside of your showcase room, so people passing by will see them.

If you get a booth, you will also want to put one in there. You want it to be large and have a visual impact. We moved our tall floor banner between the booth and the showcase this past year, for each of our two nights of showcases.

INCENDIO
MODERN WORLD GUITAR
INCENDIOBAND.COM

Figure 4 (previous page): Incendio banner for WAA

You will need to bring your best game face and get ready to talk, listen, and get to know people. Each conference has different social events that are set up specifically for artists and presenters to meet and for artists to meet other artists. There is a mentoring program for newbies, where you are paired with a seasoned pro and can ask them questions before the conference, and at the little breakfast gathering the day that the marketplace opens.

Sometimes meeting other artists can be as important as meeting presenters. Some artists are happy to share their contacts in exchange for contacts that you may have in other areas. You may also meet artists that are happy to put you up for a night or two if you are touring near them. Then there are just some fantastic friendships to be made when like-minded people with common interests spend time together. Some real lifelong friendships have sprung up from these conferences.

Let's say you have committed to a booth in the "marketplace" or "floor," or whatever the conference decides to call it. In this booth, you should have cards or flyers, banners, and some device playing a live video of your group. You will need to provide headphones so people can listen, as there is no amplification allowed on the floor. We use a headphone distribution box (like from a recording studio – usually attached to affordable headphones), so numerous folks can hear at once. Sometimes there are several folks from one venue; sometimes, there are folks from different venues listening together. Maybe you want to have some swag to give away, such as pens or stickers. Agents and self-represented artists almost always have candy or mints or some other little snack at their booths. Always be creative. IMPORTANT: having electricity at your booth is NOT a given. You have to order it, and depending on the venue, it can be an extra charge. But if you want to use more than your laptop, say a computer, a big screen, and headphone distribution box, make sure you indicate that you want electricity in your booth!

If you are with an agent, the agent will have the booth and be representing all of their artists in the booth. As an independent, you will have the booth and be representing yourself. It's important to note that if you are with an agent already, or manage to secure a temporary non-exclusive agent who will be at the conference, you can be in the marketplace (though not necessarily always hanging out in their booth – be respectful!) by purchasing a "day pass" that is available to agent's artists so they can attend. If your agent agrees to it, you can get a full 3-day artist pass for $245, or a one-day pass for $145. This can help bring your costs down considerably, while still giving you some "face-time" in the conference so prospective bookers can see your smiling face. So that's one possibility for reducing your cost.

Besides the evening showcases, during the day, there are a variety of panels and discussions by professionals teaching about different areas of the business. There are bookers and promoters telling you what kind of pitch they find most compelling.

They will tell you what sort of EPK will catch their attention and the type that they will disregard. Other people will talk about block booking, promotion, and different facets of touring. You will have the opportunity to learn about many aspects of the business over three days that can help you become more effective at getting gigs, touring, and other opportunities that you didn't even know existed.

The only way to learn about these is to jump in and get your feet wet. Yes, you will make mistakes and come away going, "shoot, I wish I'd brought or done this or that," but the only way you learn is to go.

So now that you know some of the mechanics, let's go back and discuss a little more about the conferences. APAP is the biggest and happens at the beginning of the year. WAA happens in September and is not as big as APAP, but is still pretty huge with many national acts and venues represented. Also, the showcases are all usually contained there at one location, unlike APAP. There are acts, presenters, and agents from all over the USA and the world at APAP. WAA tends to lean towards the western USA though there are some international and east coast reps for sure. These conferences are quite costly and represent everything from ballet, opera, large stage acts, bands, dance troupes, solo theater works, comedians, and singer-songwriters. I wouldn't advise jumping in full force and spending a ton of money for your first time, but it may work for you. Our first conference was WAA, and we were a bit overwhelmed! On the other hand, if you have a team and you go in prepared and perhaps get selected for a juried showcase, this could be a great opportunity. A lot depends on the substance of your act.

There are a variety of regional conferences that are very good for bands, as their focus is not so much on huge acts such as ballet companies or international acts that feature many people in their presentation. These are Arts Midwest and Arts Northwest. These conferences are not as costly, and you have the chance of more regional presenters seeing you. These also have lots of learning opportunities going on throughout the day. You can introduce yourself to many of the presenters, agents, and other people who are part of the workshops and symposiums. Many of these conferences offer block-booking opportunities. Block-booking is where venues pool their strengths to provide groups with a two to four-day package of shows – each venue will pay a little less and be able to guarantee you more overall.

Folk Alliance is just for musicians and yes, mainly folk acts – it is honestly a wonderful musical experience. You don't have to play strictly folk music, but earthier and more intimate groups are embraced. These promoters also love guitar pickers! At the larger conferences, there can be some very big presenters that don't want to be bothered by the "smaller acts" - they are on a mission to pick the best, most explosive big stuff, and can sometimes seem standoffish or unapproachable. This tends not to be the case at Folk Alliance. You can chat them up in the hallway at Folk Alliance - if they think it would be a good fit or not, they will tell you. Folk Alliance is a fun conference, where song breaks out everywhere!

Note: JP sez "attending this conference is the first time I ever strongly felt that I had found 'my tribe,' people that just were consumed by music for music's sake, and that was something that was valued by the prospective bookers."

Now, even if you can't afford a showcase or to go to any of these conferences, there are benefits to joining the organization that puts on the event. Becoming a member gives you access to the presenter list (also made up of organization members) with their contact information. You can call and email them directly, let them know you are a member of the affiliated group, and make your own presentation.

There are many ways to get involved with the booking conferences. We have seen artists that started a guerilla showcase room just for themselves and performed on and off all day. They created a fantastic light and art show behind them that was going on during every performance. These pals are called Terra Guitarra, and Bruce and Julie are another excellent example of artists who took their own destiny into their hands and made it happen. http://www.terraguitarra.com

There is another interesting possibility, and this is a good one for tribute acts. We will speak of this particular event in Los Angeles – you will need to look to see if your city sponsors a similar function. Concertshare is a one-day event that usually takes place in Diamond Bar, about 20 miles east of Los Angeles. It usually happens in January. Very little is online regarding this event, but Facebook usually has one dedicated page to it that updates in the early fall. Concertshare hosts bookers from cities in and around Los Angeles, most of whom are looking to fill their summer concert series. Concertshare typically costs about $125 to present. They are often looking for tribute bands or other types of cover acts, but they do have occasional slots for original or more unusual acts. There are presenters and buyers from each city. They usually have a good handle on what type of musical acts their community enjoys, so that is what they look for. You will have to poke around the internet a bit for the contact info since it's a small event and the contact changes from time to time.

Thanks to the internet, you can LOOK to see who played in last year's series in each city. This is critically important information – consult that concert list to see if your music fits – if not, don't waste their time, and critically, don't waste YOURS!

At this Concertshare event, there are no showcases. You have a booth with all your material, which should include a video with headphones for potential bookers to be able to listen to your act. Similarly, there is no live audio allowed in any of the conference rooms. This is, of course, out of respect for everyone there, so that there is a level playing field for the performers. Your video can be playing all the time, and as long as the screen fits in your booth, the size is up to you. Having your video running constantly is an excellent way to catch the attention of prospective presenters. You also want to have fliers, banners, and swag that you can pass out. Like at the larger booking conferences, some folks just bring a laptop, but some set up large TV monitors attached to either their computer or a DVD player, for better visibility.

The presenters will be walking around, so again be prepared to participate in a lot of friendly and informative discussions about your group. Pass out your card and anything else that will help them remember who you are. You also want to write down all of the presenter's information and follow up with them about a week after the event. They may love your act, but these presenters see so many different acts throughout the day, and at other events, that a friendly reminder is a smart and very acceptable protocol to follow. I have heard far too many musicians complaining about calling a venue or a presenter and they never called back. It would be nice if everyone called back, but that's simply not a reality. You could speculate all day on why they didn't and take it personally, or you could not take it personally and simply call again. For better or worse, these people get inundated with lots of calls, emails, and bands looking to get booked. Some people mean well but just are overwhelmed and forget. Some people are just not very friendly or responsive, and that is in all areas of life - again, you shouldn't take it personally. The old adage "the squeaky wheel gets the grease" is still very true. It's a balancing act of being respectfully squeaky to stay in people's minds without driving them crazy. So set yourself reminders to send the occasional email or the phone call to remind them that you would still love to be a part of their series, and if not this year perhaps next. If you do this long enough, you will come to see what level of "follow-up" best suits your organizational skills and schedule.

Ultimately, ALL BOOKING is about making relationships and being consistent.

There are similar conferences to Concertshare all over the country. They are specific to different regions, and you can often find out about them through the local government and or community offices. They often work off of local grants or community/chamber-of-commerce funding for their cities. That is why during recessions, these types of concerts series often go away – they lose their funding, and sometimes don't ever get it back.

Another way to find different performance venues is by searching for a summer concert series in a particular area. Sometimes you find a database - other times, you will find a list. These are usually park concerts that are also funded by the city. You have a built-in audience as they typically attract local families that want to enjoy music in a friendly, family environment. They sometimes have a decent budget, and the audience will often buy band merchandise. These are commonly referred to as "soft-ticket" shows, where you're not responsible for bringing a huge crowd, though obviously if you can get people there, it helps your presentation and reputation with that promoter for the future.

The Levitt series is also something to look into. There are Levitt Pavilions all over the country as well as extended Levitt AMP series. The primary Levitt venues (such as the ones in Los Angeles, Westport CT, Memphis TN, Arlington TX, Dayton OH, and Sioux Falls South Dakota) are beautiful refurbished (or in some cases rebuilt) band shells. They then bring in music, sometimes five days a week, in the summer. These are great local community events that attract all sorts of people, including families that want to have a fun night out with the kids. These are free events where people can sit outside, eat, and hear music. This is also true of the Levitt AMP venues. These are places that win matching grants from the Levitt Foundation to put on shows for their communities. There are 15 Levitt AMP winners every year, usually announced in late December. For 2020, they include St. Johnsbury VT, Berea KY, and Merced CA, amongst others.

Many of the different summer concert series, including the Levitt venues, have their own sound systems and built-in audiences. You typically play either two 45-minute sets or on 90-minute set.

So now that you know what you need in your booking toolbox and you have all these great leads on how to find venues, you need to start putting it all together.

Side note: as we delve deeper into individual coaching, we make an important point over and over. It's obvious but always bears repeating: make sure to be polite and friendly when reaching out. These people get lots of musicians and others reaching out to them, so be the person that they enjoy talking to, not the one that they are desperately trying to get off the phone. How often should you follow up? Ultimately you'll develop a feel for this. It shouldn't be every few days. Some folks won't want to hear from you soon; others won't mind.

Philosophical side note:
Confucius — 'The green reed which bends in the wind is stronger than the mighty oak which breaks in a storm."

Translation = you are better off as a small plant. No, seriously, now - sometimes, you just have to be flexible. Not wishy-washy but understand that there are several different roads to your destination. If one isn't working, then try a different path. It's been said that artists take chances for the rest of the world. Others may watch and wish that they could play that instrument, write the song, or travel around the world - for many, that is not their calling. So they live those dreams vicariously through working artists, the musicians that create the soundtrack to their lives.

If you lose your job as a banker or an insurance salesman, you probably won't go home and start banking or selling insurance. However, as artists, if we lose a particular gig, we will still go home and play music and create. It's what we do and who we are. Music and art are critical to our society all over the globe, whether some choose to acknowledge it or not. As musicians, we are sensitive creatures, and that's what allows us to write and play music. It is important to honor that gift. I have seen far too many musicians have their dreams and aspirations yanked out from under them.

Whether it was because someone new came into the record company, or someone at said record company decided to use the group as a tax write-off instead of promoting them, the effect it has on that artist is the same. Whether it was because the style of music you are playing is not in style anymore, or you lost your deal and don't know what to do next, the loss of that dream has had a devastating effect on all artists. Some bounce back better than others - some never bounce back at all.

Some let their gift die, and in so doing, part of them dies with it. That path you went down was just one road. It might have felt like the ultimate road, and at times the only road, but it was just one road. There are many other roads, but your anger and grief over the crumbling of your current road might blind you. Take some time to feel bad, cry, break a few things, and scream. Then regroup and find that other path. Your song, your voice, and your music might be the inspiration and the medication that someone needed to hear. Or maybe it was the song you needed to sing just for you. Life is not a smooth ride. If you allow yourself to bend and flow with the ever-changing tides, then like the green reeds, you will bounce back. If you view your art as something that needs to be heard and will touch others, then you need to get it out there. There is no need to let the gift of your music die because of a particular turn of events.
The music is inside you – it is part of you. Please remember this.

Chapter 4
How to book a tour

There are many moving parts to booking a successful tour. When I say successful, I mean coming home with money in your pocket and not too stressed out. That means that you have got to do a lot of investigative pre-booking work. There are always going to be those surprises and road bumps for which you did not plan, so you want to do your best to minimize those unforeseen upsets.

Here's some basic math to keep in mind. You are trying to make a living, so you need to make some money. It is hard (but not impossible) to make money doing one or two shows in an area. It is a little easier to make more money if you can work regionally, do several shows within a 2-3 hour radius, and drive back to a hotel or perhaps a friend's house to sleep. Our band has successfully toured for years with this in mind. It looks like the band is out for a long time, but really, the band's longest tour has been three weeks. More often, we fly, do a small group of gigs, then return home, then do the same thing the following week. Staying out there in a van constantly, like for 2-3 months, can be really back-breaking and expensive. It puts a lot of strain inside the band and with spouses and families. Be aware of the many stresses that can befall you by going on a lot of these marathon show runs.

Now, you've got some options as to where to book yourself. If you follow the Incendio methodology, you will be booking yourself at a festival first, or at least trying as we do! But you can certainly use a club show, or coffeehouse show that pays (especially if you are a single or duo act, and plan to drive to the show instead of fly) the same way. This is to say, you are trying to get an "anchor date," where you get one solid, good-paying show and build other shows around it. Let's say you live in Colorado and get a good show in Bangor, Maine. Your first foray into making a "tour" might be to look in surrounding areas of Maine, possibly even nearby New Hampshire, Vermont, or Massachusetts. You want a situation where you can perhaps drive 2 to 3 hours to your next destination and play. Any more than that, and you're courting exhaustion, a delay from traffic accidents, and any of several other small problems that can block your way (more on this shortly).

In the fall, winter and spring, it is generally more challenging to line up weekday shows. In the winter when it's cold, you might be asking new possible fans to come out when it's freezing and not easy to get to the venue. U2 can probably make that happen, but it will be harder for you! Bands that already live in colder areas, like the Midwest or Canada, know how to navigate the cold and still have their fans come out. During the summer, cities usually offer summer concerts in the park or similar, and those often happen on weekdays. These shows provide the best opportunity for you to extend your run of shows. Regardless, if you can put together a weekend run of two or three shows, or if you can start mid-week and go through the weekend in a specific region, you could be doing very well for yourself. Generally, the best time to try this is the summer. Mid-spring (before colleges have finals) is another good time to try to book a few shows. And the summer festival season usually extends into mid-October as the weather is still decent in most states. There are some great October festivals around the country.

Once you have an anchor date and start setting up other shows, it becomes super important to consult your maps again. As you are plotting your course across the country, it helps to have a map out so you can get a visual on where you are going and see the distances between the different venues you are calling. Then you want to plug those locations into a map app (like Apple maps or Googlemaps), so you have a realistic idea of the distances that you are planning on driving or flying. One of the most important things is to give yourself a realistic time frame to get from one place to the next. Know and understand your geographical location and all the idiosyncratic issues that belong to those areas. Traveling four hours to get to a show in Kentucky is not the same as traveling four hours in New York. You need to know that it may take you eight hours or longer to go what looks to be only four hours on the map. There is lots of traffic in certain areas and sometimes only one road that gets you there. If there is an accident, you are in trouble! Remember to consider a possible alternate route when planning your tour.

We all want to maximize our time out on the road to make it as lucrative as possible, but don't screw yourself in the process. Take your time when you are going into a new area. Do as much research as you can. If the route you chose to drive looks too windy and circuitous on the map, you might want to travel another way. Those types of long drives on a windy road especially at night can be very stressful, and if there is no way off the road and there is an accident that blocks both lanes it could keep you from making your performance or from getting much-needed sleep after the gig (sometimes before the gig). Both situations are a real drag!

Traffic in big cities is something you seriously need to consider. Our band has been stuck on the George Washington Bridge in NYC multiple times at different times of the day. So when you are planning out your tour, try to be as realistic as possible when you are in the process of routing. Sometimes we all have to suck it up and drive crazy distances to the next gig because that's just how things worked out. That is also the reality of touring.

My first touring experience was in a Winnebago RV with the 80's metal band Vixen. Our routing looked like a child had scribbled across the map. We drove long distances after the show and slept in the Winnebago. We would often arrive at the venue the next day in time to soundcheck, eat, and perform. It happens, but it's not sustainable, particularly as you get older in your playing career. So anything you can do to minimize that craziness will go a long way towards keeping a relatively sane and healthy band, or at least a sane and healthy YOU.

Booking hotels or rooms to sleep is something else that takes time but is essential for the health and well being of your group. Using Priceline has been an invaluable tool for us in booking Incendio. You can often get three to four-star hotels for the same price you would pay for a one to two-star if you called them directly. There is nothing like a good night's sleep and a nice shower in a clean hotel to change or maintain people's moods. Touring can be tiring and stressful - you want everyone at their best for the show. So if you do plan to visit budget motels, make sure you book at least a few decent hotels and spend a little more along the way – it will help band morale and attitude tremendously and show that you care as a bandleader. Airbnb's are also a good option to research in some areas. There are always new companies like these popping up, so do your research and stay aware of deals that are out there. I encourage you to use them to keep your costs down and experience up. Remember when we were talking about meeting other musicians at booking conferences? This is where you might take that person up on their offer to stay at their house. Sometimes sharing some food, wine, and conversation with someone outside of the band is a nice break. Also, people that live in the area can let you know about possible future venues, local restaurants, coffeehouse, or the best routes in and out of town.

If you are flying, try booking flights early. This will help to get you the best price. Sometimes the ticket price will go up overnight, and that will adversely affect your bottom line. Keep watching for a decent price and take advantage of that when you see the price for the tickets go down. A good and well-known rule of thumb is that fares tend to be the lowest about between 50 and 60 days before your flight date. However, if your tour dates come during a holiday like Labor Day or Easter, you will definitely have to buy your ticket before the 60-day mark to ensure a reasonable price and availability. Now, truth be told, even with your research, sometimes the prices go down even further and sometimes back up again. You have to start developing some intuition about when to buy. That comes with practice and experience, but you have to jump in to learn. Sometimes the price is going to go down even further right after you purchased your tickets. It happens – it's part of the gig!

We all know how difficult traveling with our instruments has become. Some airlines are better than others. I hesitate to recommend any because they are always changing their policies, or someone buys one of the existing airlines and changes everything. I will tell you the airlines that we have had the most success with as far as bringing our instruments on board with the least problems. Southwest has been very nice for us well as Delta, but not always.

Here are some tricks. Pay a little extra for the early boarding to make sure you get on right after the first class and special needs travelers. It will get you closer to guaranteeing your instrument a spot in the overhead bin, and that is what you want. If you have several people carrying instruments, stay together, and put all of your instruments in one overhead compartment. We can get two nylon string cases next to each other and put a soft-shell bass or guitar case on top. That way, you can point out that your instruments aren't taking up any more room than other passenger's baggage if anyone asks. This is, however, a constant struggle and can cause stress. The less conspicuous you are, the better and always do your best to be friendly and polite. Asking beforehand is not particularly a good idea. Just board and try to draw as little attention to yourself as possible.

Some people choose to get a good road case and check their instruments, but the airlines still manage to break them - we've seen it happen too often. There is the possibility of your instrument not making it to the next destination. That has also happened to us and others that we know. It is a real problem when you have a performance that evening and no instrument! Then you are on the phone calling around trying to rent or buy something at the last minute. Not fun! If you find that you have arrived at the gig, but your instrument has not, often the first call you should make is to the venue, and particularly the soundperson of that venue if you have that info. They will usually be the first in line to lend you a decent replacement instrument for the night. Many of our colleagues, and ourselves included, do our best to bring our instruments on board the plane and put them in the overhead to avoid precisely this situation. You're taking a chance no matter which way you decide to go.

Now let's talk about which airport you are going to fly into. This choice will affect how much you are going to pay for your rental car. The difference between renting a car or van in NYC or Washington DC is quite a bit. If you can fly into a smaller city to start your tour, like Baltimore, you can often save a lot of money on the van and car rentals. We have found that it's usually cheaper to rent a car or van in a smaller city. It's often also less expensive to rent in the city than at the airport. You may find that an Uber or Lyft ride to a car rental plus the cost of that rental will be significantly cheaper than simply getting the vehicle at the airport, especially if the rental is for several days or several weeks. If we as a band find this to be the case, we will fly into an east coast airport (usually somewhat late in the evening as we fly out of LAX) then take the shuttle to a nearby airport hotel. The next day, one or two of us will get up and take an Uber or Lyft (or even sometimes the hotel shuttle!) to the lowest-cost rental place, drive it back to the hotel, and collect the band to start the tour.

Sometimes it's cheaper to rent two smaller cars than one big van. This also causes two people to drive and costs more in gas, but even with that, it can sometimes be less expensive, especially when you are talking about one of those big gas-guzzling seven or twelve-passenger vans. Again, do your research and cost analysis. Wisely choosing which airport to fly into can save you a considerable amount of money.
You need to make sure to keep all this in mind when routing your tour. You can even try Rent-A-Wreck if you want to take a chance, but I have to say our experience with them has not been great, especially in Washington DC, where you can get a cargo van for

less money. Then again, others have used them, and it's worked out fine, and helped the band's bottom line.

If you have to rent gear, spend the time and arrange that long before you leave. Many stores now rent gear too. Call and price out gear in the local music stores or places that specifically rent musical equipment and shop for the best price and gear.

Make sure you give the places you are renting from the exact specs you want for your gear. Then if they don't have what you request they will tell you what is available and you can make an informed decision. If you say "I need a drum set and bass amp," and they give you something you don't like you have only yourself to blame – this goes back to the "stage plot" issue from chapter 1 – you have to do some research and find out EXACTLY what your band needs, and come as close to it as you can.
One person's Ferrari is another's Yugo. Not everyone likes the same thing.

Now, on the other hand, if you request specific gear and you confirm those items with the rental company, they should have those items when you arrive. If you show up and they don't have what you need, you should have your email confirmation in hand to prove the discrepancy. They will either change it if possible, not charge you as much, or at least feel bad, so you have some leverage if you have to bring the gear back a little late or when you work with them again if you choose to do so. Once at the rental place, take a moment to open everything up and make sure it's all there and generally in working order. The worst thing is to pick up all your equipment, get to your show, and only then discover that there is no speaker cable from the bass amp to the speaker or no hi-hat stand. Take the time and open everything up. You will be glad you did.

Do you have an endorsement deal? If so, speak with your artist representative and see if they can help you out by setting you up with an amp or drum set for the tour or part of the tour. If you are going to be going to several separate locations (for instance, in and around New York for a week and then flying into the Chicago area for a week), let your artist rep know and see if they can help you out in each place.

Philosophical side note:
This is an opportunity to make new friends and enrich your life.

As you are calling and making these different arrangements, you have the opportunity to make a network of new friends. Although all these logistics that go along with booking a tour might take you out of your comfort zone, it is an excellent opportunity to forge new relationships. Having a network of people you can trust and who are familiar with you and your needs can make touring easier and more enjoyable. You may find someone at a car rental in Wisconsin that you always speak with when booking your tour. You might develop a good relationship with the music rental company in Chicago. You can build a friendly relationship with these folks, and they, in turn, can recommend you for gigs or festivals or new gear, as well as make the trip smoother by having one less item (namely decent gear) to worry about.

As you build these relationships, it not only benefits you, but you will develop a database of people and companies to recommend to others. You've already found who is reliable, so if another musician is asking for a referral, you have someone and someplace to send them. You are building a network and building goodwill by helping both parties.

If you don't take a few moments to find out about the people with whom you are working, you might be missing out. You and the person booking your flight or club owner might share other interests. Maybe you love philosophy, yoga, or cooking, and you find they do as well. You can turn each other on to books, podcasts, or people that you hadn't heard of before. Perhaps they may have just watched a video on marketing that is just what you needed to see.

Many individuals have a deeper well of knowledge then a surface encounter will reveal. This also establishes another line of communication between both parties. You have made an enjoyable and memorable experience out of what could have been an uninteresting encounter. Of course, we don't always have the time to explore these relationships, but just approaching each encounter in an open and friendly manner can have a subtle but very impactful way of affecting your journey.

Chapter 5
Questions you need to ask the venue

First of all, you need to develop your own contract. You won't always use it – venues often like to use their own. But you should know the working parts and have one ready to go if requested.

Below you'll find a sample contract, loosely based on what we use for Incendio and Carbe and Durand. This is NOT a standardized contract – every single one can and should be tailored to the requirements of the show. Sometimes our tech rider is quite extensive if we agree to a concert, just to make sure they have the equipment we need – NEVER ASSUME, WRITE IT DOWN! But this will give you a basic outline of some of the items that should be considered. I would say that of the 150-180 shows that we do a year with both our large group and the duo, about 30% require a contract similar to this one. For the other 70%, the venue promoter generates the contract.

INCENDIO MUSIC
PERFORMANCE AGREEMENT
900 Spanish Way, Weirdsville CA – (xxx) xxx-xxxx

This contract for the performance on the engagement described herein is made this 5th of February, between the undersigned purchaser of live music performance (hereinafter called "Purchaser") and the music group Incendio (hereinafter called "artist").

Venue:	The Green Meadow Ampitheater
Type of Show:	Park concert
Date:	Saturday June 27, 2020
Times:	showtime 5 to 7pm Load-in: 3:30pm; soundcheck 4pm Two 50 minute sets with 10 minute intermission

The attached rider is hereby made part of this contract and must be signed by all parties:

Lights and sound:	Purchaser to provide in accordance with rider - please see tech rider
Accommodations:	4 non-smoking hotel rooms, each with one king or queen bed
Amenities:	N/A
Wages:	$x,xxx
Capacity:	1,200
Ticket scaling:	N/A
Gross potential:	$x,xxx

It is hereby agreed that collective group known as Incendio is an Independent Contractor and not an employee of the undersigned Purchaser

Regarding merchandise sales, artist shall be allowed to sell audio tapes, Compact Discs and/or other promotional materials – revenue split as set forth in the rider below.

Hold Harmless: Purchaser hereby covenants and agrees to save and hold the artist, its subsidiaries, affiliates, officers, directors, shareholders and employees free, clear, and harmless of any and all liability, loss, costs, expenses including attorney's fees, judgements, claims, and demands of any kind whatsoever in connection with, arising out of, or by reason of any act, omission or negligence of Purchaser or its respective agents, employees, servants, or contractors in any way connected with or arising out of an accident, injury, or damage, whether to person or property, whatsoever occurring before, at, in, upon, about, after, or in any manner connected with its service to artist.

89

This contract is binding per the laws of the state of California. The signatures below confirm that the parties have read and approved each and all terms and conditions contained herein.

Purchaser: Incendio (authorized signatory):

_____   _____
Green Meadow Holdings   Jean-Pierre Durand from Incendio
Attn: Jack Smith   900 Spanish Way
3200 Hearst Avenue   Weirdsville, CA 91746
Anywhere, CA 90032   XXX-XXX-XXXX
jsmith@example.com   Federal Tax ID for Incendio: XX-XXXXXXXX
XXX-XXX-XXXX

INCENDIO RIDER

MAIN BAND CONTACT: JP Durand XXX-XXX-XXXX or info@xxxxxguitar.com

ADVERTISING:
• All shows must be billed as "Incendio" unless otherwise noted.
• Incendio's music shall be referred to as "World Guitar" unless otherwise
agreed upon.

MEALS:
• Four hot meals or equivalent access to food during event. This would include a salad,
standard meal of proteins, veggies, and some vegetarian options.

BACKSTAGE/HOSPITALITY:
• A dressing room with locking doors, makeup lighting, mirror, electrical outlets, and hot
and cold running water.
• Clean bathrooms inside, adjacent, or at least near dressing rooms.

• Four (4) bottles of water
• 4 clean small towels for after show.
• 4 complimentary passes to event for band guests.
• complimentary meal for the group after the concert.

PAYMENT:
• payment to Incendio immediately at the end of performance.
• All checks shall be made out to Incendio Music.

MERCHANDISE:
• Green Meadow staff will sell merchandise on behalf of Incendio, adding state sales tax
as applicable. Green Meadow will then retain 10% of net sales and remit to Incendio
remaining 90% net sales at end of sales period this same evening.

BACKLINE:
Incendio is comprised of 2 guitarists, a bassist, and a drummer. The guitarists
hear themselves through the monitors only, so their mix is critical – but they do
not require any additional amplifiers. We will bring bass amp and drumkit.

Any problems or issues in fulfilling this rider shall be discussed and negotiated prior to
engagement and preferably when contract is signed. For production questions and/or
publicity materials, please contact JP Durand at XXX-XXX-XXXX.

_____   _____

Purchaser   Incendio

In your contract, you should state the amount you are getting paid, how much is the down payment, or the deposit, if any. Are you asking for a third of the fee as a deposit, or one half? Or will the venue pay the full amount the day or night of the performance? Every venue works differently. You'll want to ask: what time is load in? Soundcheck? And the show? What time do the doors open? This question often translates to "how long do we have for soundcheck?". How long are you playing, and how many sets? Will the venue provide rooms, dinner, backstage food and drinks? If you are at a festival, are they providing food backstage or food vouchers? Do you get free or a discount on drinks and food if you are performing at a club or restaurant? Will sound, soundperson, and backline be provided? If you are performing outside, is there a covering from the sun or rain? All of these concerns have to be stipulated in your contract and signed by both parties. It doesn't always guarantee you will agree on everything, but you should put as much in writing as possible. This way, your chances for disagreement are minimized - if there is a serious problem or breach of agreement, you have a document to prove it. You don't want to get into "he-said-she-said." You want a written document that you can present if there is a problem. Usually accompanying that contract is your rider, which states very clearly what you need and want. This as well as the contract may differ (and can easily be modified) for each venue depending on what they can or cannot provide.

So the basic rule you want to live by is <u>Assume Nothing</u>. When you book your shows make sure you speak directly to someone, preferably the promoter (to get directions, maps, and to be told specific things of which to be aware for that particular venue) and, possibly closer to the show, the sound person (to confirm soundboard, mains, monitors, backline if needed, types of microphones available, all of the technical specifications of the show). You want to speak with someone that knows exactly what equipment they have at the venue. Confirming that they have a PA is not enough. Ask what kind of speakers they have for the mains and the monitors. What kind of board do they have, and how many inputs? How much power per side does the power amp have? You need to be very specific! Not so long ago, we did a show where the outdoor venue had a rinky-dink PA and no microphones or mic stands! The show, the last one to be added to the tour schedule, was a low-paying fill-in date and was confirmed at an airport when we were headed to a different show several weeks before. I had not done the proper follow up, and we got burned.

If they have backline, ask for the model of the bass amp and any other amps they have. Make sure to ask what kind of drum set, how many toms, what sizes are the toms, and what kind of drum throne, amidst other questions. Is the drummer expected to bring his or her own snare, cymbals, kick pedal? You want to know as much as you can so that there are no unfortunate surprises when you arrive. You want to be very insistent about speaking with the soundperson, as they will give you the best information. The best sound people will be HAPPY to talk to you – they also want the show to go well.

If you speak with someone that works at the venue, books the venue, or is any other way affiliated with the venue, they may have all the best intentions but simply don't know about sound equipment. They may believe that a small 30-watt amp with a Shure 58 on a mic stand is a PA. A drum set with a throne that could double as a torture device and a hi-hat stand that has a broken pedal may not be what you need to put on a show with your six-piece band. If you are not diligent about asking all of these questions and the equipment at the venue is not adequate, it's on you. If you've asked and they give you a written confirmation regarding the sound equipment at the venue, you can decide if that will work for you or if you will need to bring or rent additional equipment. If, upon your arrival, you find a discrepancy between the equipment they have and the equipment you were promised, you should have an email with your confirmed equipment list. In the end, you just want to put on a good show. Asking all these questions will help you achieve that goal.

You will also need to develop an intuition about checking on equipment. There will be some places that, for whatever reason, just can't seem to give you a straight answer, or the answers they give you seem squirrely. If you are worried about the equipment and you can bring other gear with you, it's better to play it safe and bring it along.

While you are learning all of these situations, it's good to have a list of questions to help you remember everything to ask. There is a lot! Here's a brief checklist for a small quartet indoor show with 100 to 200 people:

1) what kind of PA do you have? What types of mains (the main speakers) and monitors (the little boxes on the floor that allow you to hear yourselves)? A good rule of thumb is for them to at least have an 8-channel board, as well as an amp that can deliver at least 500 watts a side into speakers that can receive 500 watts a side. Newer speakers often have the amp inside them, like a QSC K12 or a JBL PRX815W. Having a pair of these, hopefully with an appropriate matched subwoofer, would be suitable for a small concert. Outdoors, two speakers on each side for a total of 4, plus subwoofer, would be preferable.

2) How many monitors do you have? And SUPER-IMPORTANTLY, how many monitor mixes do you have? The drummer typically will not want to hear the same thing as the vocalist. For a quartet, do they have four individual monitors with four individual mixes? Is there separate EQ on those monitor mixes?

3) Do they have mics and mic stands? Do they have cables?

4) How many inputs do they have on their board? Eight channels are a decent amount with which to start. For smaller rooms or rooms that obviously cannot support a drum kit, a 4 or 6 channel mixer to accommodate just vocals might be okay even with a drumkit – you just have to make sure the PA carries ONLY vocals and maybe an acoustic guitar or other acoustic instruments.

For guitar amps, what do they have? A Fender Deluxe often works well in a smaller room. A combo bass amp from Ampeg, Fender, Mark, or any of a number of other reputable bass amp companies should be fine. Hopefully, your drummer is bringing his or her own set, but if not, and there's a house set, what are the tom sizes? Are the heads fresh? If not, and you break a head, does the venue carry spare heads? Little things like this can make or break your show.

Philosophical side note:
Socrates: Know Thyself

Having a strong sense of self (without being an arrogant jerk) and a clear vision of your artistic voice will help you weather the many turbulent waters of being an artist. It's one of those elementary things to say, but you spend a lifetime trying to achieve. There are so many things that sway you this way and that.

Whether it's out on the road with a group of people that you are trying to fit in with, or a producer that you aren't sure if you like, but you were told you should. It's confusing! To which inner voice should you be listening?

You have to know what it is you love. Even if it's some obscure form of music that most people don't know. If that's your voice and that's what speaks to you, then be true to your muse. If you spend your time chasing the newest trend because you want to be successful, you are going to lose yourself in the process.

Find your voice and stick with it. If you succeed or fail from one day to the next, it will be easier to know that it was and is something that you are passionate about. If you fail to do something that you didn't like to begin with, it's seriously going to suck. If you succeed in doing something that you have no passion for and are stuck doing it for years, it won't be the path you were hoping for. If you love what you do, others will feel your enthusiasm, and you will find your tribe. Love what you do; be focused!

Chapter 6
Understand stage sound and the crew at the venue

When I was touring with Leon Patillo (Christian artist and former Santana singer), I learned a very valuable lesson from a choreographer by the name of Vince Paterson. Vince had done a lot of choreography and dance and had worked with all sorts of well-known artists such as Michael Jackson and Madonna. He was brought in to work with us on simple dance steps while we played and sang. I had fun working with him on the choreography. But his most valuable advice had nothing to do with dance. He said to make sure you introduce yourself to everyone and thank everyone after the show.

I have done my best to always follow that advice. As musicians and performers, we need to remember that this is a team effort. The sound, lights, crew, promotion, venue, and anyone else involved want and need to do their best to make a successful event. As performers, we can get very self-involved and forget that everyone else involved in the evening is also a trained professional to varying degrees. Some are better than others; some are nicer than others. But being mindful of being friendly and respectful to everyone involved will make your performance more enjoyable for you, the other performers and the audience. Acknowledging and thanking someone for their work on even the smallest of things goes a long way for establishing a good relationship and making that person want to work harder for the event. Feeling appreciated is usually something that makes people want to do their best! That is a good thing all around. You can help make a fun and happy environment by bringing that attitude with you to every show.

I'll give you a scenario. The sound crew is generally educated in their field. They have to deal with many moving parts (both in terms of equipment and others on the crew) that can fail and stop working at any time. If you are performing at a festival and the crew have had to get five bands before you on and off stage, the crew might be a little irritable. If the band before you were jerks to the crew, they may not be feeling very amicable towards musicians. If you go in, introduce yourself with a smile and ask their names, that action breaks the ice and establishes you as someone that cares about them. Remember that if you choose to treat them disrespectfully, they are not as inspired to work with you, and they might even compromise your gig! This is a team effort, and you want everyone on your team to be working hard for a good performance. People paid to come to this event or at least took time out of their day/night to be there. Playing music is also something you are passionate about, or you probably wouldn't be doing it. So you want to do everything you can to put on a good show.

Now, let's talk a little bit about understanding sound. Having an understanding of how sound and equalization (also known as "eq") works will make life easier and more enjoyable for you and the sound crew. Understanding the basics will make a world of difference. If you can't hear your kick drum, maybe it's an eq issue. Perhaps if you want drums in your monitor but they are boomy, and you can't hear yourself, you'll want to ask the soundperson to cut maybe some 250 Hz (which is where there is a lot of low end "woof") and bring down the guitars in your monitor. This can "clean up" your sound, perhaps making it easier to hear yourself. Maybe as a guitarist with an amp, you might want to help your bandmate by facing that amp in a different direction and bring the volume down. Perhaps the bass needs to add some high mids and cut some lows on stage to help get a cleaner onstage sound and allow the mains to carry the low end. You need to know not to aim your mic into the monitors or cover it with your hand, or an annoying and possibly hearing-damaging squeal will scream out of the monitor. For guitarists, understand that because your amp sounded good in the club last night does not mean that the same settings will sound good in the venue tonight. Every stage and PA system has a different sound and needs to be approached as such.

Being able to speak to the sound crew and convey what you need in an educated manner will ingratiate you to them. They will appreciate that you took the time and energy to learn your craft. If you go into a venue and start yelling that you hate the way your monitor sounds or start randomly turning up without taking any of these other parameters into account, your relationship with the sound crew will be much more difficult. Your performance will not be as enjoyable or go as smoothly as it could have. Take time to learn a little about all aspects of the business you have chosen.

When you are soundchecking, go one by one. The leader of the band should establish how this needs to be. Let each person test their sound, then speak directly to the sound person to get their instrument/monitor sounding the way they want it, then go on to the next band member. Sometimes the soundperson takes control and lets you know who they want to check and in what order. If that works for you, then just follow their lead. Your soundperson can only focus on one thing at a time. If everyone is telling them what they need at the same time, it can make their process much more difficult. Of course, if something is screaming loud in your monitor and deafening you, it needs to be addressed right away. Much of this may seem obvious to some of you, but for many, it isn't. If you incorporate these concepts into your touring and performance practices sooner than later, you will have a much more enjoyable time performing and touring.

Now, you are going to encounter sound crews and people that just have a bad attitude. That's life, and you have to do your best. Developing strategies is helpful so you are not caught by surprise when it happens. We have dealt with more than one soundperson who seemed fine when we first walked in, then by the time soundcheck rolls around, they were either drunk or possibly jacked up on meth or just weren't as pleasant as we first thought. At this point, someone in the band has to delicately step in to "assist" this person in the most diplomatic way possible to make sure that the gig still happens and that everyone sounds good. This is yet another great reason to know your sound and to know how EQ works!

If one of us is talking to the soundperson and we notice that they don't seem to like or respect us for whatever reason, we send another band member over. Some people still have their strange types of prejudice (like some don't want to talk to the "girl" in the band and get bent out of shape no matter how vast her experience). We are there to put on a show and not get in a fight. Each band develops its own internal codes for different problems. With just a little smile or raised eyebrows, we let our band members know there is a problem, and someone else takes over.

Philosophical side note:
There is an African saying, "Hold an egg too tightly, and you will break it, hold it too loosely, and it will slip through your hands."

Have you ever heard a rough demo someone made of their music and thought it was amazing, and then you heard the finished recording and thought that it didn't measure up to the demo? Have you ever recorded fifteen takes of a song or one track and realized that the first or second take was the best? Have you ever recorded a part that sounded technically perfect, but in listening back, you realized it didn't have any magic? In a quest for perfection, sometimes we lose focus along the way or lose sight of the whole because we get so obsessed with tiny details.

Sometimes those obsessions have more to do with our fear of putting something out there in the world to be judged, or our fear of failing. So instead of seeing our stalling tactics for what they are, we convince ourselves that the last take just wasn't good enough. One of the favorite lines people use that are too scared to finish is that they are perfectionists and won't settle for anything that isn't perfect. I've met a lot of those people along the way. The one thing that they have in common is that they never finished their project or that they produced every bit of magic and life out of their music.

Of course, there is always the other extreme of people who should have spent more time on their song and craft but are blissfully unaware. But that is for another discussion. You have to give yourself permission to fail, succeed, and, most importantly, grow. You'll never know, and you'll never get better or get feedback if you don't eventually release your music.

I have friends who have recorded their albums several times because it just wasn't good enough and then just gave up. I have listened to people record multiple takes, none being appreciably better than the last only to abandon their project. A producer friend once gave us great advice as to multiple takes of a song, or a solo, or a vocal: "ask yourself, are you making it better, or are you making it different?". It's an excellent standard to judge, and the quicker you realize it, the easier it will be to make artistic decisions.

If you don't give yourself the chance to fail, then you won't allow yourself to succeed. Jump in! The water is always changing.

Chapter 7
Stage and Backstage etiquette

So at this point, you may be thinking, really? I'm polite. What's to know?

Let's talk about backstage first. The way you conduct yourself around the promoters, bookers, and other people that may be backstage can affect whether or not you will be hired again. Remember: promoters talk to other promoters as does the crew, helpers, and other people backstage. You don't know who is back there! A kid carrying your towels may be the daughter of the promoter or the club owner. If you are acting like a jerk, you can be sure they will hear about it.

Some things I've seen people do, I wouldn't have even thought about until I saw them do it. For example, if you are at a festival and there is food backstage for everyone, you do not want to use your hands to grab the salad or dump your soup back in the pot if you don't want anymore. You might be thinking, "that's ridiculous," but I assure you it happens! Also, try not to go back for thirds and fourths. There are many more hungry musicians waiting to eat. This might sound like basic manners and etiquette, and it is, but you'd be surprised how many people do not seem to have a handle on basic manners. Being on tour for weeks is no excuse.

You don't want to insult anyone backstage, either. If you need to say something unfavorable about someone at the venue, wait until you are back in the hotel where no one can hear you. Many gigs are lost because someone in the band said something unkind about someone associated with the venue. This exact scenario happened to a bandleader friend of ours, and there was severe damage control required to stabilize the relationship with the promoter. Remember that promoters will share this experience with other venues, and then those people will be reluctant to hire you as well. If you must say something about someone that may be offensive, do it in private and keep your voice low!

Philosophical side note:
Don't get lost in the minutiae.

Identifying and understanding the big picture of what you are trying to achieve is paramount to your success. If you (or a collaborator) get hung up on small details that are not that important to the big picture, you can find yourself getting bogged down and not moving forward. There is a difference between minutiae and the critical points, and you need to learn how to identify the difference.

One of our early production gigs was working with another producer. He had a contract where we had to reproduce popular songs of the day exactly as the original but at two different BPMs (beats per minute). They were for aerobic classes, and they wanted them for high and low impact, so they were very specific about the BPM. That gig taught us several techniques. Because they were very dense tracks that we were reconstructing, we had to listen very carefully to identify and reproduce each sound and performance.

It was quite tricky, but we learned so much and have been able to apply that knowledge to our future projects.

The other thing we learned was to stay on point. After the producer hiring us heard our work and knew that we had the credentials and skills to do the job, we got together to talk. He said, "I need someone to do this job in this way. I'm not interested in your artistic preferences. If you think this is silly and you want to argue with me about your feelings in regards to this project, then you won't work out. If you have a hard time dealing with all the different vocalists that you need to hire, I don't want to hear about it; you just have to make it happen. I need someone to do this job exactly as I'm asking you to." The man was on point and concise. As a result, we were clear on the goal, allowing everyone to get the job done.

Identify what your end goal is and don't get sidetracked with things that keep you from achieving that goal.

Chapter 8
Creative ways to promote your shows

There are many different ways to help promote your shows and social media. If you are a young fresh face, then you have probably grown up with a world of social media, and most of your friends populate Instagram, Twitter, and even TikTok. Life moves so fast these days that those platforms may be passé by the time this book is published!! If you are older and work in folk/rock or any style that might appeal to an older audience, then Facebook is probably for you.

Facebook posts are very valuable, but you need to consider promoting your posts (and using Facebook ads) and put some targeted money behind them. There are parameters on Facebook that allow you to target specific regions that you will be visiting. You can also access certain types of people by age, by interest, and by geographical area, among many other factors. Music lovers are, of course, one of the first groups you would want to target. If you are playing mellow music or jazz, you might want to target the winery crowd. If you are playing rock, you can target people that are into electric guitars and drums. You have to research the style of music that you play and the people that enjoy your genre so that you can direct your ads to that audience.

There are two different kinds of promotions offered on Facebook. Promoted posts and boosted posts will show up in your news feed. These posts are primarily directed towards friends who are already in your feed. You can use these posts to let your audience know about an upcoming gig or new album.

Ads will show up in the upper right-hand corner. These can be used to introduce your product to potential new supporters who aren't friends or fans yet. This is a good way to further distinguish between the two types of promotions: https://www.facebook.com/business/help/3170830 72148603

These types of ads are also available on Instagram, which has grown to rival Facebook in terms of ads due to its popularity and high level of engagement. Not surprisingly, Facebook now owns Instagram.

If you have a Twitter following, then make sure you tweet with a video to get people engaged and let them know where you are going to be. Maybe you want to record a lesson to get people's attention. Perhaps you want to make a video that shows you in the studio working on a new song, or doing something funny on the way to your next show. If you post engaging content, both diehard fans and casual listeners will be interested in finding out more about you.

If you want to develop your twitter strategies, we highly recommend our friend Madalyn Sklar at https://madalynsklar.com/

STREAMING OPPORTUNITIES

If you are an artist whose music is streamed on Pandora, take advantage of Pandora Amp and The

Next Big Sound. You can record personalized ads that will stream before one of your songs is played. And it's FREE. It's a great tool to help promote your shows as well as any other projects you may have.

People that have heard us on Pandora are always showing up to one of our Incendio shows. This phenomenon started a few years ago and has grown tremendously. These fans often let us know that they heard us AND our ad on Pandora, and that's why they came to the show. We have acquired many fans over the years using this invaluable tool. Even if your song is playing on another channel, your ad will run. There are many other tools available to artists who are streaming on Pandora, so make sure to research and utilize these tools to maximize your impact.

Spotify also allows you to run ads that help promote your shows. Additionally, you want to make playlists (that include your music, of course) that can be shared on your social platforms along with reminders about your upcoming shows. Reaching out to local businesses before you come into town and asking if they will play your music in their store or restaurant is also useful. You can send them a CD, a USB stick with your music, or simply ask them to play your Pandora or Spotify channel.

You can also see if those businesses will be willing to put up a poster in their window to promote your show. If you have fans in a town that you are coming to, you can ask them to be your street team and hit some of the local venues with your posters and fliers. You can also reach out to local newspapers and ask if they will include your event in their entertainment section or the local events. It would be good to talk to the promoter of the club, theater, or concert series that you are performing at; you want to see where THEY think a poster or other promo would be most effective.

Contacting local radio stations or public radio can be beneficial - most of the stations are happy to help you promote your show. By supporting your band, they are also supporting the community.

Sometimes you can also get on local TV stations. Yes, this is a lot of work! But local/regional programming on morning shows can be great for generating interest in your event. A good promoter will provide you a list of radio, television stations, production companies, and press opportunities when you confirm your show.

You can't do it all, but you can try some of these approaches. So knowing what's out there and available to you will help you make informed decisions. The promoters are always happy to see you show initiative to promote your shows. Promoted posts like the Facebook ones we described above also can be part of an overall promo strategy that gets folks to your concert. The promoters love seeing that as well, and the more folks you can get to your shows (even a soft ticket show), the more CDs you can possibly sell, and the more you will spread the word about your band.

<u>Philosophical side note:</u>
Take a moment to reflect on and enjoy your accomplishments.

The continuing laundry list of tasks that we need to do is never-ending. The minute we finish one job, there are hundreds more that need to be done, especially as an independent artist. Standing back and taking note of what you have accomplished is a grounding and productive exercise. It will help give you the energy to move forward. To be clear, I'm not talking about making a couple of phone calls, surfing the rest of the day, and then congratulating yourself for a job well done!

However, if you have completed a song, an album, booked a successful tour or gig, or achieved something that you have put some real work into, then get into the habit of giving yourself time to reflect on the fulfillment of these goals and celebrate them. It's part of enjoying the process and generating more enthusiasm for moving forward with your next task. It also gives you a good opportunity to review and see what you might do differently to make life easier the next time around.

You don't need to rest on your laurels or run around bragging. Just take the time to give yourself some props. Looking back over the past year or several months and focusing on what you've achieved is a healthy thing to do. It can be very invigorating.

It also provides some needed perspective. If you feel that you have not accomplished what you set out to do, take the time to examine why. What didn't work? What can you change to be more effective? If there is someone that you trust with whom you can review your decisions, that could also bring some much-needed perspective.

Chapter 9
Royalties

Note: one of the main objectives of this book has been to put things into a practical context. I wanted to keep things simple while giving you real-world information, not something that was written by someone that "used to do this stuff" or someone that studied but never actually did anything in the real world. So when it came to this chapter, we were in a bit of a quandary. Our first stab was reasonably simple. Then after reviewing what we wrote, we decided that we needed to elaborate in more detail to make sure our readers didn't miss anything.

Luckily for you and us, my cousin Jennifer Cary happens to be an expert on royalties and is the founder of Sovereign Music Services, which is now part of InGrooves. Jen and her team are instrumental in making sure that musicians get paid their royalties. Yay! She's the woman with the knowledge and the answers. We wanted to leave no stone unturned as far as royalties, so we ran the chapter past her.

After she went through everything and gave us her notes, we realized that there was no way to simplify this subject without leaving out essential details.

Yikes! We imagined our readers' eyes glazing over as we were writing it all down. I thought of many of you saying, "I just want to get paid and get back to writing music." We totally got this! We decided to summarize the chapter first and then go into the details. This way, you will have a list of all the organizations you need to join upfront. Then you can start digging into the nitty-gritty reasons as you go. So here it is!

PROs (PERFORMING RIGHTS ASSOCIATIONS) - ASCAP, BMI, and SESAC.
You must join one of these as a writer. If you own your publishing company, register it with one of these PROs. These companies collect your writers and publishing royalties. You can join ASCAP and BMI on your own. You must be invited to join SESAC.

https://ome.ascap.com/
https://www.bmi.com/join
https://www.sesac.com/#!/

You must join SoundExchange to get your streaming royalties.

https://www.soundexchange.com/

You must register your works with HFA Harry Fox Agency and Music Reports to get your mechanical royalties.

https://www.harryfox.com/#/
https://www.musicreports.com/#

You need to join MCPS/PRS or GEMA to get your mechanical and performance foreign royalties that are not collected by some of the other organizations.

https://www.prsformusic.com/join/writer/join-mcps
https://join-gema.de/

Now there is your list, and you need to join or register with all of them. If you want to know why then continue reading, and it will all be explained, links given, and perhaps a cocktail suggested after you read through this several times.

OK, NOW THE BASICS

You're heading towards being an independent musician. You want to understand and be able to generate multiple income streams. One of those income streams is generating royalties. These sources include:
• Record company royalties
• Mechanical royalties to the publisher/songwriter
• Sync licensing fees
• Performer-writer royalties from a performing rights society
• Performer-publisher royalties from performing rights society
• SoundExchange royalties from streaming services
• Streaming mechanicals
• International royalties from various organizations
• Print music royalties

Whether you sign with a record company or start your own, you will need to understand how musicians are compensated for any music sales. If a label sells your music, that's a contract. If someone asks you to use your music in a film, TV show, or commercial, that's a contract. You need to learn as much as possible, and this chapter will provide an introduction. It's complicated! Take your time with

116

the material, and consult the links at the end of the chapter.

RECORD COMPANY ROYALTIES

My music lawyer cousin, Jenn Cary, explained a simple bedrock concept you need to remember. Everything starts with one fundamental action: you write your song. That's creation. You own that song. Everything that happens AFTER that is a business transaction: to whom do you assign your master recordings? How do you negotiate with a publisher to represent that song on your behalf? How does that publisher compensate you and himself or herself from any usage/placement they may achieve for your song? And so on.

What does this mean? Again, per Royaltyexchange.com: "Music royalties are generated for the use of a copyright. And every song has two copyrights attached to it—one for the song as written down (the composition) and one for the song as recorded (the recording). Songwriters earn royalties on the composition copyright, and performers earn royalties on the recording copyright." ALL SUBSEQUENT ROYALTY PAYMENTS THAT YOU CAN RECEIVE BEGIN FROM THIS SENTENCE.

Once released, the song will generate revenue:
• via folks purchasing the CD, vinyl or download, or listening online.
• via radio stations and non-interactive streaming services that play the song.
• from the use of a song in a film, TV show, or some

117

new media.

Let's start with the CD, vinyl, or download. There are two key revenue streams that have to be paid by the record company: to the publisher/songwriter, and to the recording artist. The record company must pay a mechanical license to the publisher of the song for the right to reproduce that song mechanically (meaning on a CD, on a record, on an 8-track, or cassette). This is from the first CD sale, or first paid download or first stream. Simultaneously, the record company also must pay an agreed-upon rate per track to the recording artist (not the songwriter/publisher) for that master recording. So the songwriter gets paid, and the artist gets paid. This division is critical to understanding where subsequent monies come from.

Some initial observations: the more independent you are, the more those revenues come back to you IF you can effectively promote your music, and folks become aware of it. Also, you can see that while the record company might at some point pay the band or artist once their "recoupables" are covered, the songwriter (via the publisher) has to be paid from day one. You can imagine how lucrative this can be for the songwriter, and why they often do better financially than the band recording their song. This is a good argument for writing songs within a band! However, the band does have one advantage – they can go out and tour, and thus make money that is not split with the record company or the publisher! In doing so, they will almost certainly promote whatever song is on their album – in that way, a songwriter who is not in the band will benefit from a band touring and promoting his or her composition.

It's essential to know a little general history of how this all started. When a record company signed you (when records were the PRIMARY way that the general public listened to music), for every single record they sold, they would owe the songwriter a compulsory mechanical royalty rate. From 1902 to 1977, that rate was 2 cents per reproduction per song. Changes in the Copyright Act of 1976 modified that rate to "2.75 cents or 0.5 cent per minute of playing time or fraction thereof, whichever is greater". In 1980, via the 1980 Mechanical Rate Adjustment Proceeding, it went up to 4 cents – through the years, it was raised continuously. By 2009, the royalty rate had reached 9.1 cents. You can find out more at:
https://www.copyright.gov/licensing/m200a.pdf

From 1902 to 1977, you'd be seeing the transition from Edison cylinders and sheet music only, to the gradual prominence of records (first 78's on shellac, then vinyl). Cassette tapes and 8-tracks soon followed. Starting in the '80s, the record companies transitioned to CD's as vinyl gradually disappeared. For both vinyl and later CD's, there was a giant distribution network of middlemen around the world who purchased vinyl and CD's from the record companies at wholesale rates, then distributed them physically by truck to record stores. The more prominent artists would be able to negotiate better royalty rates from their record companies. The artist would receive a small record company royalty for

CDs sold, usually at 10% to 25% of the suggested retail price. This later changed (of course) to 10% to 25% of the wholesale price.

The reason it is called a "compulsory" mechanical license is that the record company OWES it to the songwriter/publisher, by hook or by crook. The mechanical royalty, once set for the duration of that contract (or beyond if so stipulated), is fixed and is a legal obligation that the record company has to pay. This differs slightly from a record company royalty, which is still a legal obligation paid to the artist. However, if you sign your masters to the record company, or they advance you money for the recording of those masters, that will obviously be charged back to you from the money they advanced you for the recording of your music.

Now, if a movie wants to use that recording of yours, that's a sync license, and is different from a mechanical license. This can be a third revenue stream that comes into the record label, of which a portion goes to the artist. A sync license is a contract where the record company says, "You want to use a song on our label, "Bees Buzz" by the Orange Twinkles, that's going to cost you $100,000" or, perhaps if you are a lesser-known artist (or don't have a super bad-ass name like the Orange Twinkles), maybe $1000. Of course, the label contractually will keep a certain pre-arranged percentage of that money (less so if the band or artist is popular and had a lawyer who advised them well to sign a halfway decent contract). Still, again, they would owe you some money per the terms of the contract.

So those are the three ways you can make money from a record company: mechanical licenses, record company royalties, and sync fees. Hopefully, it is starting to become more apparent to you why we advocate an independent path, where you are a songwriter, publisher, label, all in one. That way, if you do well, much more of the revenue comes back directly to YOU.

Over more recent years, musicians signed to labels have learned a few other essential points. First, CD's were dying off in favor of downloads. That, in turn, has given way to streaming, which is now the primary way that music is enjoyed. And second, the record companies for years had often found many ways of "creative accounting" in the form of "recoupables" or "chargebacks" to your band account. The record company MAY have paid some of your tour support. But they also MAY have paid for the vice-president of marketing to go a "festive" all-expenses getaway to Bimini or perhaps paid for work on that VP's Ferrari. But as that chain of middlemen and distributors disappeared, so did the opportunity to hide these extra little "expenses." Read *Hit Men* by Frederic Dannen or *Stiffed: A True Story of MCA, the Music Business*, and the Mafia by William Knoedelseder for some juicy and gripping stories of what the music world was like back then.

FYI, these days, a far more common type of record deal is a "net profit" deal (also known as a "net receipt" deal). In this scenario, the breakdown is that the artist and the label go 50/50 on the deal, after recoupment of initial monies laid out. In essence, this is a better deal than the lower record company rate that used to be paid, but now, the mechanical royalty commonly comes entirely out of the artist's share, period. The following article goes more into good depth into this type of deal, highlighting the pros and cons from both sides:

https://blog.buko.net/legal/management-and-recording/net-profit-deals-a-recent-alternative-to-the-traditional-record-deal/

With all the head-spinning changes in the music industry over the last 20 years, we've gone from a standard compulsory rate of about 9 cents per CD to seeing CDs largely disappear from the market. For artists these days, it's all about streaming.

From a 2020 Ditto.com article, we can see the following 2020 royalty rates paid by various platforms:
Napster = $.019 per stream
Tidal = $.01284 per stream
Apple Music = $.00783 per stream
Google Play = $.00676 per stream
Deezer = $.0064 per stream
Spotify = $.00437 per stream
Amazon = $.00402 per stream
Pandora = $.00133 per stream
Youtube = $.00069 per stream
Here's the full article at Ditto:
https://www.dittomusic.com/blog/how-much-do-music-streaming-services-pay-musicians

As an example, Spotify pays .0064 per stream these days (that's a 6th of a cent). Now, if you're SIGNED to a label in a traditional record contract, as their artist, you're going to see about 10% of that number. So if you're independent, you stand to see more money. But if you don't have a label behind you, no one might hear your music, and you might not generate any revenue. It's a bit of a catch 22. But this is where you could receive some royalties for your original music if you release it for streaming on Spotify, Pandora, Apple Music, Deezer, or other streaming platforms.

PERFORMING RIGHTS ASSOCIATIONS

JP and I have written a lot of music for music libraries over the last twenty-five years. These compositions have gotten a lot of placements in shows like "Modern Family," "Burn Notice," and "Law and Order" among many others. When our music plays in TV shows or other similar situations, a performing rights society monitors that usage and pays us. How do they get the money to pay us? TV stations pay all manner of licensing fees to be on the air. That money goes out in many different directions; some of it goes to fund musicians as recognition of the role that the music plays in televised shows. If you get a small snippet of your music used in one TV show one time, you'll get a small payment for that. If you write the theme to "Two And A Half Men," and it plays continuously around the world, you're going to make a lot more money! The Performing Rights Societies, or PROs, usually pay you quarterly royalties. They scan all channels for music (a lot of which has now been "watermarked" so the PRO computers can "hear" what music has been used and then identify who wrote it). PROs also receive "cue sheets" from shows listing what music has been used. Between those two approaches, they can determine whose music has been used and for how long in each show. Then the PRO assigns that music a "value" and pays on that "value." They do the same for terrestrial radio plays.

The three primary PRO's in the United States are ASCAP (founded in 1914), BMI (founded in 1939), and SESAC (the newcomer, founded in 1940). They will collect your "performance royalties."

You can and should join ONE of these PRO's. After you join, you have to register your music with them so that they know the music is yours and they can collect the money on your behalf. You can list your compositions online through the PRO's portal after you register with that organization as a writer, and, if you are self-publishing, as a publisher. They will pay you three types of royalties:
• Writers royalties on domestic (USA) plays
• Writers royalties on international plays
• Publishers royalties on domestic and foreign plays

These different organizations pay quarterly, usually a few months after the "usage" of your music. If they did not survey the usage, you won't get paid. So it would be helpful to try to keep track of when your music is being played so you can let them know if it slips through the cracks on their part, especially if you are a smaller indie artist.

JP and I are members of ASCAP. But our Incendio partner Jim is a member of BMI. Both PROs are effective, as is SESAC. It's hard to tell if one PRO will pay you more than another – we have heard many differing viewpoints on the subject. If you have not signed a publishing deal and wish to keep your publishing, you need to start a publishing company and register your compositions with that company. Typically, you will go with one company for both the writer and publisher shares, but that's not a hard and fast rule. Some folks use one PRO for their writer royalties, and another for their publisher share.

Let's say you place a song in a movie, and you own the song. The movie plays on cable around the world, so you would receive your domestic writers royalties for the times that the movie played in the USA. You would also receive international royalties for the times the movie played on TV internationally. Finally, you'd receive publishing royalties for owning the song every time it played. It sounds a little complicated, and it takes time to learn some of the ins and outs. Don't be afraid to call BMI or ASCAP, tell them you are a new artist and would like to join. They can lead you through the pros and cons (mostly the pros!) of joining their system. SESAC is slightly different in that they invite you to join – you cannot request to join.

ASCAP charges a $50 application fee for composers to join. They also charge publishers the same $50 fee. BMI does not charge for composers to join. However, BMI does charge publishers to join: $150 for individuals, $250 for companies. SESAC's fees for composers and publishers are the same as BMI. For all three companies, there are no additional yearly fees to pay once one has joined, only the relatively small portion they appropriate from royalties collected to pay for their overhead.

STARTING YOUR OWN PUBLISHING COMPANY

Publishing companies used to sell sheet music. It would go from the writer to the publisher so that sheet music could be sold. As the music industry evolved, the publisher held the rights to the "song" itself. So the artist would generate revenue through record company royalties, and the writer would generate revenue through the song publisher. Hence, an artist can make a LOT of additional money by owning their own publishing. Many artists and groups start their own publishing company, then expand later on as needed. For now, it's good to try to start your own. If you get signed to a publishing deal, you'll likely have a team actively pitching your songs to prospective artists for them to record. But honestly, outside of country music, this practice has gotten much smaller; a lot of people are recording their own compositions now.

If you move forward with starting a publishing company, you need to pick a name and then check online to see if it's available for usage. You can check your state's Fictitious Business name online registry. You then register that name through your local government. In Los Angeles, that office is in Norwalk, CA. You can also start a preliminary California check online:
https://www.sos.ca.gov/business-programs/business-entities/name-availability/

When you are searching, you will come across businesses that will offer to do all of this for you for a fee. Once again, I suggest doing it for yourself. So make sure you find your government office and not a third party site. Each state is a little different, so you will need to find the government office/site for your state. Then you need to decide if you want to be a sole proprietor, partnership, LLC or corporation. You will need to research each of the options to see which one is right for you. Checking with an appropriate attorney or tax accountant would be a wise idea as you decide your business structure.

You'll submit this information and the filing fee, and possibly publish your business name in the paper. Not every city will have this requirement, but the city of Los Angeles does require this. And there may be other requirements in your city or state. Once this process is complete, you will be given a DBA (doing business as) number. You will be assigned a Federal Tax ID number, and you can then open a business bank account. You are starting a business so . . . (yay!) . . . now you will have to pay taxes on whatever revenue you generate.

You then register your new publishing company with your PRO. You can now submit your recordings as you would if you were a writer, except now, the publishing royalties come to you as well IF you have retained control of your publishing. Very often, the music libraries or other companies you write for won't let you do that; THEY keep the publishing. Many (including ourselves) are OK with this arrangement since the music libraries have a sales staff whose sole job it is to sell your music for usage, along with the music of everyone else in their catalog. Sometimes record companies have a publishing arm, too, and will want you to go with that company, kind of like a one-stop-shop, so they are fully invested in your future (and can keep more of the gains if you hit it big).

SYNC FEES AND LICENSING FEES

When a show wants to use your music, they often pay you a licensing fee for the right to use this piece. This is a one-time fee and has nothing to do with the royalties you receive through your PRO when the show airs. These are separate payments. This license fee is paid to the person that owns the master and separately to the songwriter (via the publisher). If you self-release, you negotiate and receive the license fee. If you are signed to a record company, they negotiate and collect the "master recording" portion of the license fee (because they own the master recording), of which they will provide a portion to you as the artist. You would then also receive the other part of the license fee, the "song" portion, to your publisher (which is you) and then the songwriter (which is also you). How fun.

Licensing fees vary wildly. Bruce Springsteen or Muse will be able to command A LOT more money than your song. And you might not even get paid a licensing fee for the usage of your song. Sometimes TV show or film producers will ask to use your music without paying a licensing fee with the promise that you will get your PRO royalties on the back end when the piece airs. Unfortunately, this practice exists. You have to weigh out if you are willing to forego your licensing fee because you think the backend royalties make it worth it for you to do this or not.

If they do pay an upfront license, it can be very little or substantial. It depends on many factors: is it a high budget production? How well-known is the artist whose music they are using? And so on.

Sync fees, in terminology, are a bit of a throwback. This was the fee that was invented to compensate the artist for the right to synchronize their music with a moving picture, and therefore create a new type of media. The proliferation of "do-it-yourself" video and the ubiquity of this type of usage means these days that for smaller productions, the master license and the sync license are usually rolled into one legal document. When this happens with Incendio, and it's an "all-in-one" contract, for let's say $5000, we will typically split it in half, giving the $2500 "master license" part to our own record company, and paying the $2500 "sync fee" to the person or persons in the band that wrote the song. It keeps things simple!

ADDITIONAL INTERNATIONAL COLLECTION

There are certain situations, particularly in Europe, where the usage of your music might also generate some royalties that are not collected by the PRO's. In Europe, mechanical payments due to the artist are collected and paid by special organizations, unlike in the USA where they are currently handled by the record companies – as a side note, the new MCL, formed as part of the Music Modernization Act, intends to take over this mechanical royalty distribution starting in 2021 – we will see how that goes.

For example, in England, there is an entity called PRS for Music, which encompasses both PRS and MCPS. PRS pays when their members' compositions are "broadcast on TV or radio; performed or played in public, whether live or through a recording; streamed or downloaded." MCPS pays royalties when their music is "copied as physical products such as CDs and DVD's; streamed or downloaded; used in TV, film or radio." Basically, MCPS collects mechanical royalties on behalf of the writer, and PRS collects performance royalties, of a particular type that PRO's won't collect. In Germany, GEMA performs similar services but is bound by German law, not British law like PRS. There are other organizations like these in territories around the world, but PRS and GEMA are the most significant players overseas. It would behoove you to join either to collect certain international royalties, possibly depending on who is the better fit, for which you could do some online research.

• PRS and MCPS descriptions obtained from www.prsformusic.com
• GEMA can be found at www.gema.de
• BUMA/STEMRA is in the Netherlands and can be found at www.bumastemra.nl

• SACEM is in France and can be found at www.sacem.fr

• BIEM is based in France but administers mechanicals around the world: www.biem.org

SOUNDEXCHANGE & STREAMING MECHANICAL ROYALTIES

In the wake of the rise of streaming internet radio, SoundExchange emerged as the company that pays for playing your masters on streaming radio, or via their self-description, "the sole organization designated by the U.S. Congress to collect and distribute digital performance royalty for sound recordings." SoundExchange receives fees from internet streaming services and redistributes them to artists and labels. They pay 50% of the streaming performance royalty to the master owner (i.e., the record company), and 45% to the featured artist. The remaining 5% goes into the SoundExchange pot for distribution to non-featured artists, aka session musicians. Do you own your master recording? If you are on a label, that label more than likely owns the master and will collect the performance royalties when your composition is played on Spotify, Pandora, and other stations. If you own the master recording, then you will get paid directly through SoundExchange, and you will make both the 50% master royalty and the 45% artist royalty. You will not receive these performance royalties unless you are a member of SoundExchange, so you definitely need to join. The PRO's do not collect these digital performance royalties.

But there's another royalty that gets paid, which is your streaming mechanical royalty – this is for the use of the song you wrote. You remember the original premise, where a record company divides incoming revenues between those paid to the recording artist and those paid to the songwriter via the publisher? In the brave new world of streaming, the "recording-artist-master-recording" part is the "streaming performance royalty," and the "publishing/songwriter" part is the "streaming mechanical" part. How and what you get paid as a streaming mechanical depends on the distinction between non-interactive and interactive streaming platforms:

• non-interactive platforms include basic Pandora service, Sirius XM, Slacker Radio, and other services where you can tune into a certain style of music but CANNOT have direct control over which artists and songs you hear. This is basically like terrestrial radio.

• interactive platforms include Spotify, Apple Music, Tidal, and other services where you can choose whichever band or song you want to hear – you have control.

This interactivity distinction determines whether you get a streaming mechanical or not. When you listen to a non-interactive platform, the situation is like that of a radio station, insofar as you receive these small royalties as you would from a radio station – via your regular PRO.

If, however, you are listening to an interactive platform, and you are essentially playing whatever you want to hear, this system is now replacing your old record player or your iTunes – you are playing songs on demand. Now, instead of owning that album or CD or cassette that you paid for, you are paying a micro-payment to have that file "streamed" into your home. That qualifies as a "mechanical" reproduction of that music, albeit an MP3 or whatever medium is being streamed out to you. Thus, a mechanical royalty must be paid to the songwriter, via the publisher.

In the case of Pandora, each play generates .0006 cents or about ½ a cent. About .0038 of that money is earmarked as a "performance royalty" that goes 45% to the recording artist and 50% to the master owner, which is the label. The remaining .0012 cent goes to the songwriter via the publisher. If the "spin" or the single play of the track is on a non-interactive platform (where the listener can't choose the exact band and song), a tiny royalty is paid via the songwriter's PRO. But if the "spin" or the single play is on an interactive platform like Spotify, then the songwriter via the publisher needs to be paid a "streaming mechanical."

This "streaming mechanical" payment is made by the streaming services to one of two publishing administrators. The Harry Fox Agency, or HFA (which was founded in 1927 – talk about rolling with the changes!) handles the administration of streaming mechanicals for the larger music publishers such as Warner/Chappell and Sony ATV, as well as many other clients. Music Reports (https://www.musicreports.com) collects streaming mechanicals for Pandora's paid platform, Amazon, Sirius XM, and other interactive platforms. You will need to register your titles with both to maximize your revenues.

You set up an online profile for yourself, and you can go in and see for which shows your music was presented. Your dashboard allows you to see your payments, how often different stations are playing your music. There are many features to keep track of your music spins. With all of these companies, you can set up a direct deposit into your bank.

We have presented a lot of information, and eventually, you must understand how it all works. If you don't, you could be losing out on quite a bit of income.

One last detail: those small royalty rates for streaming are affected by fluctuations of both market and regulation, which make it even more complicated, if not near impossible, to accurately predict how much revenue you will receive for your streams. Keep that in mind as you're yelling at the computer screen when a royalty calculator tells you that you should have been paid $62,000, but you've only got enough money in the bank for a taco and soda.

PUBLISHING ADMINISTRATION
The world of royalties is complex and arcane. It is often challenging to keep up with all the changes. Remember that the entire ecosystem of recovering your money requires record companies to keep track of sales, PRO's to keep track of usages, SoundExchange, and other entities to keep track of plays. In some cases, your payment might not come

down to a computer keeping track of your spins, but rather a flesh-and-blood human who puts together reports and info that is critical to your career.

As an independent, an important option to consider is going with an independent publishing administrator. It is nearly impossible to stay on top of all the changes, and unless you have the desire and hours to go down that rabbit hole, your time to be creative and generate your music will be impacted by all the required follow-up. We have seen that going with a publishing administrator can be a help. Rather than a publishing deal where that company is taking on and exclusively representing your catalog, you can still rep your catalog, maintain some independence, and yet still have someone backing you up to look into all the international nooks and crannies where money owed to you may be hiding. Thus far, we have had a really good experience with our friends at Sovereign, but there are so many to choose from, such as Songtrust. As an indication of how important these services can be, Tunecore and CDBaby both offer publishing administration as an extra option. You might not get the fully comprehensive service of a dedicated publishing administrator, but it is a start. Often these guys know where to start looking, and that's a large and significant job that might be best left to them as you start or continue your career.

A RECAP TO TIE IT ALL TOGETHER

Let's go back to that imaginary classic, "Bees Buzz" by the Orange Twinkles, as an example – it's just one scenario. As it happens, that toe-tapping classic is on Nefarious Ocelot Records (NOR). The song gets released and starts doing very well. It turns out that JP Durand, who is not in the Orange Twinkles, wrote "Bees Buzz." NOR sells 1,000 CD's, but the song is a much bigger smash on different streaming platforms. So,

• NOR owes the band, the Orange Twinkles, a negotiated record company royalty rate (let's say 10% of the wholesale price) on 1,000 CDs. But NOR paid for the recording, mastering, pressing, promo to radio, and maybe a bit for tour support, all in the form of an advance. These are known as "recoupables" or "chargebacks." So the Orange Twinkles probably won't see any "record company" royalties quite yet.

• NOR owes JP Durand's publishing company, Strange Tree Productions, a mechanical royalty rate of 9.1 cents for that song per CD sold, because JP wrote it. This is not recoupable and not negotiable. The record company owes this to the publisher (and thus the songwriter) from the first CD sold.

• NOR and JP's publishing company manage to work together to get this song placed in a new movie, "Frozen Fish Treats," a comedy about trained seals who try to rob a bank. This silly but sentimental instant classic does very well. The movie's producer pays a sync license fee to allow the master recording of that song to be "synchronized" with the moving images of the film. There are two components to that fee: the part paid to NOR for the use of the master sound recording, and the part paid to the publisher/songwriter for the use of the song itself.

• The movie does well. But in the USA, performance royalties are NOT paid on film in theaters. They ARE paid for movies on TV and cable. So "Frozen Fish Treats" does very well on cable. About nine months after this movie plays on every cable service, and then a cleaned-up version plays on a major network in prime time, JP Durand will see good performance royalties paid by ASCAP for this movie that played around the world. The Orange Twinkles will not see ASCAP writer's royalties from this particular song because they did not write it. Additionally, JP Durand should see part of the publishing royalties since his publishing agreement states that any publishing revenues should be split 50/50 between himself and the publishing company. The Orange Twinkles won't see any ASCAP publishing royalties either.

• Again, as a result of the movie, folks around the world listen to "Bees Buzz" on streaming services. SoundExchange will collect streaming performance royalties and distribute 45% to the Orange Twinkles and 50% to NOR (5% left over for a fund to cover unpaid royalties). Let's now assume that because the movie is so popular, folks are picking this song and this band to listen to directly on an interactive streaming service, let's say Spotify. There are streaming mechanical royalties to be paid as well. Since JP Durand is with an independent publisher, Music Reports (not Harry Fox Agency, or HFA) will collect his streaming mechanical royalties and pay them to Strange Tree Productions, who should then pay 50% share of those mechanicals to JP Durand.

TO LICENSE OR NOT TO LICENSE?

Understanding all your royalties and how each type works is the first step in making well-informed business decisions regarding your music. You will hear people say, "never give up your publishing" or "make sure you keep all of your writers royalties." Well, in theory, and in a vacuum, that might be good advice. However, we do not live life in a vacuum, and there are always other factors at play that influence each circumstance. You need to weigh all of these parameters on a case-by-case basis before deciding on how or if you are going to license your song. I am not a person that believes in sweeping declarations and absolutes. These types of statements, when scrutinized, tend to have flaws and not be fully applicable.

I have seen all sorts of different scenarios regarding artists giving up and not giving up part of their royalties. Have you ever heard the statement, "One hundred percent of nothing is nothing"? Let's examine this scenario.

If you have the opportunity to place your song in a TV show or film but have to give up your publishing or part of your publishing to do that, it might be worth it, and it might not. If you are retaining your writer's royalties, you will still get those from your PRO. If the song is streaming and you own the master, you will get paid as the master owner AND as the featured artist if you are performing the song.
You need to know what kind of show for which your composition might be licensed. Is it a popular show?

Is the show on primetime on a major network, or is it on a small cable channel at 3 am? If it's on at 3 am, is it on every day, every week, every month? Then it might be worth it. Could this lead to connections for other placements or other work? Another critical question to ask yourself is, if you don't place it now, what are you going to do with the song? You can license the song and receive your writer's royalties, and the exposure MAY drive your streaming presence, and thus your streaming revenue. Is it worth it?

If you don't want to give up part of your publishing to place your song, you will continue to own one hundred percent. The trade-off is that the song will be generating no income. So you now own 100% of a non-revenue-generating song. Your royalties are your bargaining chip, and whether you like it or not, that is reality, and the people you will be dealing with in this business know that.

Whether this is a fair practice or not, this is how the music business works.

I have seen many instances of artists not wanting to give up any part of their royalties to get a placement. These songs could have been generating some income and could have opened the door for other placements and opportunities. Unfortunately, most of those artists have done nothing with their careers or music. The songs, into which so much effort and money were put into writing and producing, generate no income for the artists and are heard by very few. On the other hand, there are situations when choosing to not go with a specific placement is the better choice.

You may have also heard this phrase: "Your song is going to look good with my name on it." Yikes! That does not sound good! It used to be quite often that, if you were a songwriter, and placed your song with a famous artist, they would be listed as one of the writers, or the sole writer, although not always. Yes, they would get part of your writer's royalties and get part of the credit for writing your song, in exchange for the publicity and money that you would make from that famous artist recording and performing your song. Maybe that artist's publisher will take part of your publishing ownership. You can be sure that the record company will own the master, and the artist will get the featured artist share of streaming. Do you think that in this case that it's worth giving up part of your publishing and writers royalties? In a lot of cases, the answer to that gamble would be a resounding yes. It does depend on the situation. The money you will make from a famous artist releasing one of your songs could be quite significant, not to mention the opportunities to write more songs for this artist or others. You must evaluate each situation by its own set of unique parameters. This situation does not happen as much as it used to but is yet another indication of how important it is to be informed on royalties, so if faced with this type of situation, you can make informed choices.

As I mentioned, JP and I write for quite a few music libraries and have many placements. Music libraries often take your publishing. That's usually how the model works. They get publishing royalties, both mechanicals and PRO money, because they have a marketing and administrative team working to place the music that you write in different productions. The success or failure of different libraries is all about their marketing team's connections and effectiveness, not to mention the quality of the library music offered. Before you write or give your music to a library, make sure they are well-established and have a good track record. We've had friends ask us why we don't try to license our music ourselves and bypass the libraries. The answer is that there is simply not enough time to do everything.

Finally, I'm going to tell you a story about my friend and colleague, Thom Pace. He placed his song "Maybe" in the 1974 movie "The Life and Times of Grizzly Adams." That movie became a television series, and then that series became syndicated. Many iterations of Grizzly Adams used Thom's song "Maybe." Let's just say that Thom hit the jackpot! Just to add a bit of drama to the story, someone offered to buy that song from him before it was placed in "Grizzly Adams." At that time, he was a struggling songwriter, could have used the money, and almost sold the song. But for some fortuitous reason, he decided against selling it. It's worth mentioning that this was in the '70s, and the business has changed dramatically since then. However, there are always new opportunities, and as I keep saying, every situation is unique. There are still opportunities to hit that "jackpot." As our friend (super-talented independent musician) Lisa Lynne Franco says, "each piece of music is a lottery ticket."

Don't pass up a good opportunity because you have received bad but well-intended advice! Educate yourself before you make a decision.

And as for that cocktail? We recommend an Old-fashioned. Or, after trying to understand all this, maybe just consider a bottle of anything - with a straw. And a pillow for your little head - hopefully soon it will stop spinning from all the new information!

Philosophical side note:
Don't look at the top of the mountain - just put one foot in front of the next.

You won't learn it all in a year. You might not learn it all in a decade. In our case, we knew we, along with our Incendio partner Jim Stubblefield, wanted to take our destiny in our own hands. But that means constant self-education. There is no "set-it-and-forget-it." When we started the group in 1999, there was no streaming radio, no youtube, almost none of the infrastructure one sees today for music on the internet.
Know that change is constant, consult with your musician friends, ask questions, and get informed.
This brave new world of music is continuously evolving. Sometimes it's super-frustrating to learn how to stay on top of one trend only to find that it's given way to a brand new direction. We used to sell a LOT of CDs at our shows – that has fallen off mightily in the last few years. Nowadays, the opportunity for

self-promotion is the most comprehensive and wide-ranging than it has ever been, but EVERYONE is screaming for attention. Do you simply scream louder? Or do you hone your messaging for your product to better serve the fans you do have, in the hopes that more like them will come along? Learning recording techniques will help you develop better habits for getting a great sound on stage. Playing more onstage will mean increasing your audience, and you will owe it to them to push the boundaries of your art when you record. Do you see how it's all interactive? Recording feeds touring, touring feeds writing, writing feeds recording, and thus the cycle of (hopefully) growth continues. All of these disciplines need to be nurtured. It's hard for one to thrive in one aspect of the music business without the others if you wish to be a self-reliant live musician promoting your own compositions. Every show is a learning moment, as is every second in the studio. Enjoy it, take notes, give yourself a break, and know that it probably won't happen overnight. Moreover, know that your work brings joy and comfort to so many, and ultimately brings joy back on you many times over. Try to nurture that covenant.

Note: this was the section in the book that required the most research, and is only intended to scratch the surface. I used the following as references, and you should check them out when you have a moment: https://iconcollective.edu/how-music-royalties-work/

https://www.royaltyexchange.com/blog/mechanical
-royalties#sthash.jE91F5Lh.dpbs
https://blog.songtrust.com/types-of-streaming-
royalties
https://diymusician.cdbaby.com/music-
rights/collect-royalties-pandora-plays/

Chapter 10
Copyright and Trademark

I just want to mention a brief overview on these aspects. You do need to protect your intellectual property. You should copyright your music and, if possible, trademark your band name.

Copyright Office
https://www.copyright.gov

You can copyright your songs, instrumental music, collection of songs or soundtracks that you have written for movies. Just create an account at the Copyright Office.

They have excellent tutorials that will take you through the process. You can usually get someone on the phone pretty fast to help clarify anything that you don't understand. I have found the staff at the Copyright Office to be very helpful and pleasant.

There are mixed feelings about copyrighting your songs if you have already released them on an album, published them with your own publishing company (or someone else's publishing company), and registered them with your PRO. Some people feel that this is enough to prove that you are the rightful owner of your material. Other people think that you need to copyright your material to be protected; they believe having copyright gives you that extra legal protection if someone steals some of your music. It is up to you to decide what you would like to do. That being said, it's better to be safe than sorry. Spending a little extra money and time from the start could save you a lot of time and aggravation later on if there is a dispute. We are providing the link here so that if you so choose to, you can do it yourself. Some people and companies will offer to do the copyright for you, but I encourage you to save the money and do it yourself. Learning and understanding the process by creating your own copyright is empowering and educational. The more you know about all aspects of the music business, the less likely you are to have someone take advantage of you.

Trademark Office
https://tsdr.uspto.gov

If you want to Trademark your name as it relates to your band or business, you can do it online at the Trademark official site. Like every other step in this book, it's a process that you have to learn, but this site helps you through each step.

You may be asking, "what is the point of trademarking my band/project name?". Well, you have spent a lot of time developing your brand, your logo - maybe your logo is your name. Your fans have come to identify you with that branding. Then, another company comes along and wants to use that same name or logo. Now that branding that you have worked so hard to develop is getting mixed in with this other company's products. Maybe this other company has a lot of money and is now going to sue you for using the name that they want and the one you have spent years establishing. The difference is they trademarked the name, and you didn't. Now you have to change your name and remove all of your material. Getting a Trademark for your brand is a bit expensive, but it could save you MUCH more money in the future if you take the time now to properly protect yourself.

Some lawyers will offer to do this for you, but I suggest spending the time to do it yourself. Once again, you can learn how to get a Trademark, and in the process, you make sure that it's done correctly. The people at the Trademark office are very helpful, so if you have any questions as you are going through the online application, you can call them to clarify.

Philosophical side note:
Enjoy the ride and take it all in

If you have some modicum of success, you will see that keeping a successful music business means that you're going to go through a lot of ups and downs. If the music you make strikes a chord with the public, you will get taken on a bit of a roller coaster ride. But the coaster always slows, and there is someone else waiting to get on the ride. Savor the moments, the trips with bandmates seeing events, and places that few people get to see. Sometimes being a band means you get a passport to a secret, never-ending party of artistic expression, a secret hole-in-the-wall restaurant that a promoter will take you to that you would have never found on your own. It's frantically checking on your wife or husband or kids or parents from an airport gate before the next adventure. I can remember when I realized a humbling truth – if you are lucky to do this, you get interwoven into the fabric of people's lives. We were in Santa Fe, New Mexico. Despite its Southwestern vibe, our band has never been particularly embraced by that city in the same way that we have at, say, Albuquerque, where we've played many great shows. But we were playing a little club in Santa Fe, and a young man came up to me after the show. He told me that he loved my composition, the Incendio song "Loretana," and it was one of the last things he ever shared with his beloved grandmother before she passed on. He had brought his whole family to the show to meet us and thank us for making his grandmother so happy. No amount of money equals the emotional high of knowing that you provided the soundtrack to a very intimate memory, and someone thought enough of your music to let you know that it made and makes a difference in their lives.

This career path, however long or short your experience of it may be, is a noble endeavor. Learn what you can. Competition with your fellow players, sometimes so tempting, especially for younger players, is a fruitless exercise. You stand more to gain by asking questions, by helping others, and by creating a community. You'll find this path much more rewarding as you travel down this road. Cheers, and keep rockin'!

www.ingramcontent.com/pod-product-compliance
Lightning Source LLC
Chambersburg PA
CBHW061146040426
42445CB00013B/1578